NIGEL
MANSELL

By the same author:

MICHAEL SCHUMACHER
Defending the Crown

AYRTON SENNA

AYRTON SENNA
The Legend Grows

JAMES HUNT
Portrait of a champion

GERHARD BERGER
The human face of Formula 1

AYRTON SENNA
The hard edge of genius

TORVILL AND DEAN
The full story

TWO WHEEL SHOWDOWN!
The full drama of the races which decided
the World 500cc Motor Cycle Championship
from 1949

GRAND PRIX SHOWDOWN!
The full drama of the races which decided
the World Championship 1950–92

HONDA
Conquerors of the track

HONDA
The conquest of Formula 1

NIGEL MANSELL
The making of a champion

ALAIN PROST

Patrick Stephens Limited, an imprint of Haynes Publishing, has published authoritative, quality books for more than a quarter of a century. During that time the company has established a reputation as one of the world's leading publishers of books on aviation, maritime, motor cycle, car, motorsport, and railway subjects. Readers or authors with suggestions for books they would like to see published are invited to write to: The Editorial Director, Patrick Stephens Limited, Sparkford, Nr Yeovil, Somerset BA22 7JJ.

NIGEL
MANSELL

THE LION AT BAY

Christopher Hilton

Patrick Stephens Limited

First published in 1995

British Library Cataloguing-in-Publication Data:
A catalogue record for this book is
available from the British Library

ISBN: 1 85260 531 6

Library of Congress catalog card no. 95 76127

All photographs are courtesy LAT except where stated.

Patrick Stephens Limited is an imprint of Haynes Publishing,
Sparkford, Nr Yeovil, Somerset BA22 7JJ.

Designed and typeset by G&M, Raunds, Northamptonshire
Printed in Britain by Butler & Tanner Ltd, London and Frome

Contents

Introduction and acknowledgements

THIS BOOK IS a direct successor to my earlier study of Nigel Mansell (William Kimber/Corgi). It covers the period from 1992 to May 1995 — seemingly the end of his Formula 1 career. These three and a bit seasons are among the most amazing any driver has known. They embrace the unique feat of winning championships on both sides of the Atlantic and holding both at the same time. The lad from Upton-on-Severn who, early on, many judged a loser, bestrode the Atlantic Ocean, no less. These seasons also embrace bitterness, rancour, mega-dollar scheming, triumphant exile and painful, saddening return. I have tried to recreate 1992 and 1993 in great detail because they deserve it.

My thanks for help or plain speaking to Frank Williams, David Coulthard, David Brown and Ann Bradshaw of Williams Grand Prix Engineering; Bob Walters, Director of Public Relations at Indianapolis Motor Speedway; Raul Boesel, Danny Sullivan; Murray Walker and Jonathan Palmer of the BBC; Dennis Vitolo; Jim McGee, formerly of Newman-Haas, now Paul Patrick Racing; Jocelyne Bia of McLaren International; and Keke Rosberg.

I've leaned on the *Marlboro Grand Prix Guide*, the *Autocourse* annuals and TAG Heuer/Olivetti timings. I'm grateful for the services offered by Michael Knight of Newman-Haas, Proaction, the Texaco Valvoline Information Bureau, ICN and Avenue Communications.

• CHAPTER ONE •

Over
and Out

DEEP INTO MAY 1995 the new beginning became an end. Amidst
the tug and heave of events that challenge credulity, amidst the
shriek of headlines and the emptiness of guarded silences, a handful
of words came back to me. They'd been spoken years before by the
noted racing car designer Harvey Postlethwaite. 'Everybody exits
Formula 1 out of the back door, you never exit out of the front. It
doesn't happen, even to Mansell, whoever . . .'

That Nigel Ernest James Mansell made his exit out of a very large
back door didn't negate the truth of the words, although
Postlethwaite can hardly have envisaged it happening as it did. No
Formula 1 career had risen so high and degenerated so quickly into
such purdah and paucity.

The final announcement, only two days before first qualifying for
the Monaco Grand Prix, was couched in PR-speak, perhaps all that
remained. At least the agony of waiting wasn't prolonged into
Monaco.

Ron Dennis, the Managing Director of McLaren International,
who'd offered Mansell the new beginning (for a reported £7 million),
said, 'The performance of the 1995 Formula 1 car, MP4/10, has not
met the expectations of both parties so far this year. Nigel has not felt
confident within the car, and this has affected his ability to commit

The return of 1995 inevitably carried memories of other, greater days.

fully to the programme. In these circumstances, I believe that we have determined the most appropriate course of action. The relationship has been short and has obviously not achieved the results anticipated by either party. However, I have found Nigel to be entirely straightforward and totally professional in his business conduct. Whilst this decision brings to an end our current relationship, I would certainly not preclude us working together in the future.'

Mansell said, 'I am obviously disappointed that the relationship with McLaren and Mercedes [the team's engine supplier], which could have achieved so much, has been concluded early. At this stage in my career I had expected, on joining McLaren, that the total package would have given me the possibility to be competitive with the other top teams. I have certainly enjoyed many aspects of my relationship with the team and working with them has been a unique experience. They are undoubtedly building a future which will, I am sure, be successful in the long term. I have no immediate plans in Formula 1, but have welcomed the opportunity to keep in touch with the team, with whom I have parted on the best possible terms.'

And that was it, a twist to the tale.

Hadn't Mansell The Immense ridden back across the Atlantic to save Formula 1?

Initially, mind you, it had seemed simple, itself a dangerous thing to say. To recap: the 1994 season ended in Adelaide in November — Mansell won the Australian Grand Prix — and the next chapter seemed partially written already. Past 40, he'd stayed fit and lean but softened some of his edges to the point where people spoke of their delight in working with him. During 1994 he'd contested the IndyCar championship in the United States, but after the death of Ayrton Senna at Imola in May, also guested for the Rothmans Williams Renault team at four Grands Prix. Formula 1, the world's most exotic activity, needed Mansell as much as it can ever need an individual, and certainly Mansell wanted Formula 1. He'd sign a full contract with Williams and have a proper run at the 1995 championship. That simple.

Frank Williams is habitually hesitant about negotiations and, with potentially the best car, could afford to be. Others waited on him, not he on them. He played the field at his own pace. David Coulthard, 23 and with only eight Grands Prix behind him — he'd taken Senna's place until Mansell replaced him — would revert to being the team's test driver, which is what he had been before Senna's death. Coulthard had plenty of time and a twofold incentive. He was inside a great team and had every chance to follow Damon Hill, who'd graduated from testing to getting a proper Williams drive; but that was the first twist in the tale.

Coulthard is managed by IMG, an aggressive global company fashioned by the American dynamics of its founder, Mark McCormack. An anecdote about McCormack, the inventor of the sports agent, will suffice. He keeps a full wardrobe of clothes in every city he regularly flies to, so he need only carry hand luggage. He never squanders any of the minutes of his life waiting for carousels to disgorge suitcases at airports. Standing around is a violation of his natural order, as it is to the company constructed in his image. McCormack plays the field at a fast pace. Coulthard signed for Williams's great rivals Marlboro McLaren . . .

It passed immediately into the hands of lawyers, as it would, because Williams claimed that they held an option on Coulthard, but the fact that Coulthard signed for McLaren forced the hand of Frank Williams. He could scarcely deny Coulthard a drive with McLaren if all he could offer in recompense was testing the Williams. He had to make up his mind: Coulthard or Mansell. That was the second twist.

Coulthard represented an outstanding prospect — during his eight races he'd finished in the points five times, including a second place, and at the strictly commercial level came many millions of dollars cheaper than Mansell — but hadn't Mansell The Immense ridden back across the Atlantic to save Formula 1 after Senna had been taken from it? Wasn't Formula 1 convinced that only Mansell The Immense could fill the void, put the racing back into racing, pump up the televiewing figures, spice each Grand Prix with delicious, combative uncertainty?

Now, come early New Year 1995, Mansell had joined the more than two million Britons who found themselves, one way and another, unemployed. Coulthard's case went to the F1 Contracts' Recognition Board and it ruled the Williams option valid. A

Williams spokesperson voiced the opinion that 'we wouldn't have gone to all this trouble if we only wanted to have him as a test driver'. On 3 January a statement hummed from the headquarters at Didcot, confirming employment and unemployment.

'David Coulthard will be driving for the Rothmans Williams Renault team for the 1995 Grand Prix season, Team Director Frank Williams announced today. The 23-year-old Scotsman will be partnering Damon Hill driving the Williams Renault FW17s. "I am very happy we have now finalised our agreement with David. He has proved his worth as a Grand Prix driver and I have no doubts he has a successful future ahead of him," was Frank's comment.

"'I am delighted to have reached a fair agreement to race for Rothmans Williams Renault," said David. "I look forward to the hard work of the winter testing programme and the challenge of my first full Formula 1 season. I have no doubt Williams and Renault will once again produce a winning car."

'The team finished the 1994 season on a high having won the Constructors' World Championship for the seventh time thanks to the efforts of Damon Hill, David Coulthard and Nigel Mansell. Nigel won the final race in Adelaide and Frank's words of appreciation were, "On behalf of Rothmans Williams Renault we would like to thank Nigel for his contribution both in 1994 and during his 95 races with the team [1985, 1986, 1987, 1988, 1991 and 1992 as well as 1994]. We wish him all the best for the future."'

Bernard Dudot of Renault, who supplied Williams with engines and clearly had a say, subsequently revealed: 'The choice we made was a long-term choice. Frank Williams, who made the decision, was investing in the future. We spoke about re-signing Mansell but it would have been a short-term operation. I think the choice of Coulthard was a good one.'

Three days after the statement, Mansell attended a racing car show at the National Exhibition Centre, Birmingham, and was mobbed. He wore a suit, collar and tie, looked impeccably groomed, as he can. He signed a fistful of autographs and moved on to a stage where he worked the crowd, as he can. Superficially this might seem a paradox: the wealthy and untouchable Immensity who'd departed these shores for Clearwater, Florida, ought to have been remote from ordinary folk; but somehow that worked in reverse, as it always had. If he'd fled clutching dollar bills, he'd come back and here he was, among them again, re-establishing a communion with them and making them re-establish a communion with him. The wealth worked in reverse, too. He didn't have to be in a hangar at the NEC because the wealth enabled him to savour any global delight he wished, but *he was here*.

He worked the crowd by demanding of them who he should drive for. 'McLAREN,' they thundered and echoed to him. 'McLAREN!'

He sprayed champagne over them and said, 'Retirement is not a word in my vocabulary at the moment. The fire is still burning as strongly as ever. You give me the strength and will to carry on. While I have your support I will always try to continue racing. Just seeing you all here gets everything straight in my mind.'

McLaren? Here is the logic of it. Mansell wouldn't commit what remained of his career to a middle-ranking team, which left only three. Ferrari had Gerhard Berger and Jean Alesi under contract, therefore no vacancy; Benetton wanted Johnny Herbert to partner Michael Schumacher, therefore no vacancy; and McLaren, who,

Pushing it away.

courtesy of the Contracts' Board's ruling on Coulthard, did have a vacancy. That was the third twist.

Ron Dennis, running McLaren, is a meticulous man who dislikes histrionics and could not hide the fact that he had been a firm Mansell critic in the past. No doubt many at McLaren shared these sentiments: Mansell was even the butt of jokes at McLaren Christmas parties. Moreover, McLaren purrs along on harmony and even when the Senna versus Alain Prost civil war ranted and raged there, Dennis managed to sustain the dignity of the team by wielding a judicious blend of public silence or adroit public words. What might Mansell do to the purring and the harmony? He was too old, too Immense to be anything but his own man. You knew what you were getting: something strong-willed, cantankerous maybe, but a driver eminently capable of winning races, winning another championship maybe, forcing a team to ascend with him. Would Ron Dennis press down his feelings and offer the bait?

Yes.

'Our first meeting was brief and catastrophic,' Dennis would say. 'We are different characters and people knew about the opinions I had of him. At the second meeting I did some plain speaking. Nigel brings a unique style to his racing and he has a public image which is important, especially to the media. I had to look behind the split personality and I prefer the Nigel Mansell I eventually got to know than the one I had been familiar with. My attitude towards him was changed. He is committed to many things, his family and his racing.'

On 3 February the deal was announced at a kiss-and-make-up Press Conference where Mansell made all the right noises, as he can.

'I think we both learned a lot about each other we hadn't appreciated before and we like what we saw. Ron has demonstrated certain things I hadn't experienced in motor racing. He stepped in to sort out hiccups in the contract negotiations and showed himself to be thoroughly professional.'

Reportedly Mansell would be paid 10 million dollars, although in the negotiations £63,000 separated the two sides. Rather than haggle on, they agreed to donate it to charity.

'You can't stop the fire burning if it's burning,' Mansell concluded.

Right *Mansell in shadowland, 1995.*

14

'If I had done badly in the last two races of last season I wouldn't be here, but we know what happened and I am fired up now. Some will say I'm the wrong side of 40. If that is the case, then I'm carrying the banner for the over-40s. I don't have a problem with that. If you're fit enough and you look after your diet and you train hard enough and the dedication is there, and your motivation is there like it's never been before, and you can taste it, feel it, taste it, want it — if you've got all those feelings, to walk away from a fabulous opportunity like this would be wrong.'

Dennis concluded, 'I prefer the committed Nigel Mansell to the somewhat extrovert and flamboyant race-winner that I had seen up to now.'

McLaren launched their new car in mid-February at the London Science Museum, and radical it looked, even within the new, tightened regulations that had taken every designer virtually to a clean piece of paper. Mansell made all the right noises while he was mobbed again, this time by journalists and photographers. He worked them as he had worked the crowd at the NEC, happy, co-operative, proper. Posing static beside stationary new cars he could do from memory, anyway. He'd been doing it every season since 1981.

The McLaren context was much more interesting than smile, smile, smile. They'd had a dreadful 1994 by their own standards and left Peugeot to get Mercedes engines. The true quality of the car and engine would only begin to emerge in pre-season testing at Estoril. What if a dreadful 1995 beckoned? The tests were over two weeks. By a paradox, Frank Williams invited the media to the factory at Didcot during the tests — only a co-incidence — to speak of this and that, as he does each pre-season. Williams said, 'It was not an easy decision to switch to David, not an easy decision at all.' He wouldn't give reasons, although I pressed him as best I could.

You missed Ayrton the first time round (Senna tested a Williams in 1983 but they didn't sign him). Was that your thinking — that you mustn't miss Coulthard?

'I'm sorry, I don't follow your question.'

Well, you could have had five or six years of Ayrton instead of trying to beat him. If you didn't take Coulthard, were you repeating that mistake? Was that in your mind, irrespective of anything else at all?

The loneliness of the McLarens.

'We obviously think David's a bit good and we were reluctant to let him go. Ron obviously thought the same thing. I could lie to you today and say "Yeah, we've got him long-term", but we only have a one-year contract with him.'

Do you think there is still a championship in Mansell?

'Yes, certainly, yes. My worst nightmare — well, one of them — is that Nigel destroys everybody all year and we'll look a right bunch of idiots.'

Are you surprised he's come back at 41?

'He's still highly motivated to win, he's still very quick.'

While this was going on, Ann Bradshaw, the team's PR lady, fed Williams with the latest testing times as they came in. How could we know, sitting there in distant Didcot, that the fourth twist was being played out at Estoril?

Mansell first drove the McLaren there on 2 March and covered 33 laps with a best time of 1:24.37. He said, 'I managed some good runs today and I am learning a lot about the car. This afternoon I felt much happier than in the morning. A time of 1:24 isn't bad for the first day. This morning I spun [at the last right-hand corner before the pits] but 30 minutes later I was back in the car. I didn't do any damage and it was just a simple mistake.'

Hakkinen likened the cramped cockpit to running the London Marathon in shoes a size too small

---

Subsequently, strange and disquieting rumour seeped outwards, rumour that astonished — and let's be candid — amused the great British public. Mansell The Immense was physically too Immense to fit in the car! The astonishment centred naturally enough around quite how a multi-million-dollar enterprise of McLaren's expertise, experience and attention to detail could have made such an elementary error. It wasn't that straightforward, of course, because Mansell — tall for a driver at 5 ft 10 in — had signed so late, and we're talking tiny margins, but the error still seemed incomprehensible to a public who had so recently re-established the communion; seemed incomprehensible, indeed, to everyone outside Formula 1. Mansell's team-mate Mika Hakkinen, questioned about Mansell's elbows being bruised as he drove the car, said, 'Nigel is suffering more than me. His shoulders are wider and he is more heavily built.' Hakkinen likened the cramped cockpit to running the London Marathon in shoes a size too small.

A McLaren spokesman, however, soothed that 'problems with discomfort are all part of getting the car ready for the new season. Nigel had a very detailed and tortuous seat-fitting last month and everything was OK, but you cannot recreate the situation of being buffeted in the corners or braking hard and what that does to your body. Testing is designed to discover this sort of problem. It throws up other technical questions, too, but nobody seems interested in them. We may have to shave a tiny bit off the seat here or there, alter its shape slightly or move the pedals a millimetre. Either way they will be back testing at Estoril on Monday [Mansell flew from Estoril to the factory in Woking to try and help solve the problem]. It is an entirely routine situation. If this was anyone other than Nigel, there would be none of this fuss.' I assume the spokesman regretted tracts of this statement in the days to come, not least because the testing ended:

Michael Schumacher (Benetton)	1:21.30
Eddie Irvine (Jordan)	1:21.67
Damon Hill (Williams)	1:21.74
David Coulthard (Williams)	1:21.77
Rubens Barrichello (Jordan)	1:22.29
Mika Salo (Tyrrell)	1:23.10
Gerhard Berger (Ferrari)	1:23.25
Ukyo Katayama (Tyrrell)	1:23.37
Mika Hakkinen (McLaren)	1:23.51
Johnny Herbert (Benetton)	1:23.78
Pedro Lamy (Tyrrell)	1:24.06
Nigel Mansell (McLaren)	1:24.27
Pedro Diniz (Forti Corse)	1:28.72

The McLaren spokesman denied that Mansell felt such deflation with the performance of the car that he might walk away from the whole thing. 'No, that's not true. Actually, Nigel has been extremely correct. The car was plagued with inconsistent handling problems and the cause is certainly not structural.' Whatever, that was the fourth twist.

Before the first race of the season, the Brazilian on 26 March, more rumours circulated and more and more stories appeared wondering aloud whether Mansell would walk away. Certain facts emerged: he'd not be driving until a new cockpit had been made that he could fit into properly; it'd cost £350,000 and certainly couldn't be ready for Brazil or Argentina two weeks later. Mark Blundell, another Briton, was brought in as deputy.

In Brazil, Dennis said: 'It is not easy to take the public criticism that has been heaped upon us, but it is the professional thing to do. We have already built the new mock-up, Nigel sat in it on Sunday and suffice it to say you could fit a stereo and an air conditioner in it now. I am still hopeful he will be back for Imola [the San Marino Grand Prix, 30 April, third race] but we have made fools of ourselves once and I do not want to do it again. I nearly fell off my chair during lunch with Nigel on Sunday when he expressed the desire to drive the car as it was. In the end, the conclusion was still that it was not the right thing to do to race the car. The sceptics said that, if the car was two seconds a lap quicker, Nigel would have made sure he was in it, and they are probably right. But he would not have been able to do more than two or three laps. He would have tried to go through the pain barrier, but doing one quick lap and a whole race are entirely different things. It would just not have been possible.'

Mansell stayed at home while Schumacher beat Coulthard in the race, but both were disqualified, their Elf fuel declared illegal. This lifted Hakkinen to second and Blundell to fourth, which, if my mathematics are in any way reliable, was twist number five . . .

In Argentina, Hakkinen crashed at the start and Blundell's oil cooler failed after nine laps. Dennis, however, paid tribute to the professional job Blundell had done. After Argentina the FIA, the governing body, reinstated Schumacher's and Coulthard's points from Brazil, so it stood Schumacher 14, Hill 10, Alesi 8, Coulthard 6, Berger 5, Hakkinen and Herbert 3, Heinz-Harald Frentzen 2, Blundell 1.

Mansell tested a revised, 'wider' McLaren — not the new one — at Silverstone a week and a half before Imola. Work had begun on the new one on 16 March and up to 100 McLaren staff were involved. A McLaren spokesperson, Jocelyne Bia, explained that the effort 'went on round the clock with two shifts. We have managed to build two new chassis. One is due to leave for Imola on Sunday [23 April] and the other have its crash test on the Wednesday [26 April]. Assuming it passes, McLaren will race the other at Imola.' The chassis were, of course, identical, so the one to be crash-tested could be seen as representative. Not every racing car is crash-tested, or there would be no racing cars.

At Silverstone Mansell started to do very respectable times, although on his first day he needed a tow back to the pits after spinning in hail and sleet. Of the old cockpit — and missing Brazil and Argentina — he'd say, 'When you have a situation like that you

Right *Spain, the sad race. At the start he's already lost in the pack*
(ICN U.K. Bureau).

really have no feelings. You just have to deal with it, and it wasn't good. It would have been a disaster if I'd driven in those races. A lot of people think in terms of fairy tales but I look at hard facts. The facts are that certain things were not possible.' He also said, 'You cannot undo the past, but you can change the future. I would like that to be positive from here on in.'

The quickest when the three-day test finished were:

Irvine	1:29.362
Barrichello	1:29.584
Hakkinen	1:29.592
Mansell	1:30.528

He journeyed to Imola for the San Marino Grand Prix. Because the circuit had been so extensively altered to make it safer, there was an introductory session on the Thursday. Mansell spun and needed a tow back to the pits in the morning. 'It was my fault. I came out of the chicane, floored the clutch and it wasn't there. I forgot the clutch is on the steering wheel, simple as that.' He spoke these words in a gentle, self-depreciating way, and added, significantly, that in the afternoon he almost lost control of the car several times but 'was able to get it back. In the old car there was not enough room for me to do that and I would have gone off.' He paid tribute to the building of this new car in 33 days. 'Sensational.' He spoke more mutedly of the inevitable atmosphere that the memories of Senna — and rookie Roland Ratzenberger, who also died at Imola the year before — brought. 'You have to put it aside, otherwise you wouldn't function.'

In the first qualifying Mansell was ninth and, the track slower on the Saturday, stayed ninth. In the race he reached fifth but fell back to 10th after he and Irvine touched and he had to pit. He finished two laps down on the winner, Hill.

Spain two weeks later suddenly brought the end close. Mansell qualified 10th and in the race could get no higher than 13th before falling back, scrabbling over a gravel track, returning to the pits and retiring on lap 18. He gave an interview that said, in sum, that the car was undrivable. 'It's sheer understeer and oversteer, not balanced at all. I just have to go and think about it. I've no doubt whatever it is a fundamental car problem. You can make it worse or a little better, but you will never fix it. I was going to have an accident out there and that is why I came in. I am just hoping we make a big step forward because you have got to be able to trust the car. At the moment, the bottom line is that you cannot.' Then he departed. His cause was hardly helped by the fact that Hakkinen cajoled the other McLaren to a high of fourth early on and went as far as lap 53.

'We need team mates who can show their willingness to perform'

Speculation mounted, fuelled on the Monday before Monaco. Norbert Haug, the sports director of Mercedes, said, 'We need team mates who can show their willingness to perform. Mansell must help us to develop a winning car.' A Mercedes spokesman added, 'All I can say is that we saw one of our cars running towards the podium until it lost fuel pressure and one of our cars in the gravel trap.' That day, too, Dennis and Mansell attended a charity function in London and guarded their silences. 'I am not here to talk about Nigel,' Dennis said. 'You can't answer those questions. It's a shame it has to be asked,' Mansell said. Officially, however, the McLaren team insisted that 'we are still contracted to each other', and anticipated that Mansell would drive Monaco.

The back door opened the following day, the point of no return reached. As Mansell stepped through, he left a genuine legacy behind him, something both controversial and monumental and the subject of this book. Nor, surveying the scope and nature of the legacy, would you dare say that the career was truly over and the door would never open again.

• CHAPTER TWO •

The Championship Over Here

IN NOVEMBER 1992, long after the echoes of battle had died, the *Guardian* newspaper carried one of those quasi-provocative articles asking who should be President of Britain if the monarchy was abolished. Various people responded — the then Labour MP Bryan Gould made nonsense of the whole thing by stating that the Queen should become President — but Howard Brenton, a playwright, touched a nerve. 'Oh God, I think a sportsman, someone you could admire for something other than politics or brain, like Nigel Mansell, because he's just a beautiful man. The quality that is most truly British is his: bloody-mindedness.'

He'd always had that. Sometimes he'd kept it mildly concealed, sometimes he'd let everyone see it, but it had been a central constant, a core value to be drawn on like a resource or held up like a shield. The most unexpected aspect of 1992, from March to the decisive race in August, proved to be that he didn't need the bloody-mindedness except once or twice. Thereafter he drew on the resource and departed for homey Clearwater, Florida, in a mingling of fanfares, hope and, no doubt, self-righteous indignation and high dudgeon. Another chapter had closed.

The background to 1992 is swiftly told. Mansell regarded his career as a protracted struggle against odds only he could overcome and, since his entry into Formula 1 in 1980, had overcome them all except the highest, biggest and most elusive, the World Championship. Three times (1986, 1987, 1991) he'd been second, and on each of those occasions his ascent ended in a crash with no other car directly physically involved (if you get my meaning), itself a strange aspect: the infamous rear tyre blow-out at Adelaide, the crash at Suzuka in practice, the spin chasing Senna at Suzuka. No man had been second three times and not won a Championship since another Briton, Stirling Moss, in the 1950s. Was this Mansell's destiny? Moss takes a quiet, almost grim satisfaction from having finished second four times, and insists that this is such a quirk that it has adorned his fame rather than diminished it. Mansell did not intend that to happen to him.

'I'm the only driver who will go down to the racing limit with Ayrton'

Because the days between March and August 1992 fashioned Mansell into a presence even more Immense than he had been before, and because they hammered and scattered any who doubted that he had a championship in him, I propose to let it unfold by itself using what was said at the time as well as said subsequently. During those six months every single driving record (within the compass of a season) came to lie at Mansell's mercy. If he had cared to channel the bloody-mindedness into the single-mindedness of the amasser he would have re-arranged significant statistics to such a degree that they might have lasted to the turn of the century and a long time beyond.

The doubters who, circa 1980–1984, insisted that he'd never so much as win a race had to ingest the possibility that he'd win more than anybody had ever done in a season, and take more pole positions, and set more fastest laps, not to mention a host of more esoteric feats. The most points (105, Alain Prost, 1988) lay at his mercy, too, no matter that a win counted 9 points then and 10 now. A record is a record is a record. But what he wanted was the Championship, and what else arrived along the way simply arrived along the way, by-products almost.

And, at the age of 39, he was ready.

In early February Mansell talked about the season. 'I've said this

Right *The picture of 1992: Mansell alone, and leading.*

for many, many years and I'd like to put it into context as I say it today: for every team — McLaren, Ferrari and Benetton, but especially for Williams — our main competitor is ourselves [meaning you master your own machinery before you master that of your opponents]. The first thing we must achieve is reliability. If you don't have that, it doesn't matter who you are competing against. The next step is asking who is the competition? Obviously, for the last four years the opposition has been McLaren Honda [Senna champion 1988, Prost 1989, Senna 1990, Senna 1991] and there's no question that Ayrton and Gerhard Berger will be the strongest opposition. There is only one driver who is willing to go down to the wire like I am, and that's Ayrton. I really believe that equally I'm the only driver who will go down to the racing limit with Ayrton, as demonstrated at some races last year. What we've got to hope is that we both have the equipment to make some of the spectacles we made last year more often this year.'

David Brown, Mansell's race engineer — and who had first worked with him in 1985 — judges that 'in 1991 it was really starting to come together and we had a good car. For 1992 we did a lot of winter testing. We had a very good Estoril test and we did eight days. It was called The Eight Day War by the electronics guys and it was a real battle — at the beginning we were unable to do more than five laps in succession because of the problems we were having, mostly electronic.

'By the end we had a reliable, quick racing car. From there we went to another test and then off to the races: we'd done lots of homework and that was the basis of the reliability. You can have the best car in the world but if it isn't reliable you're wasting your time. Mentally, Nigel was in very good shape, very determined, driving very well. He seemed to get better every time he drove the car, be happier, and he got quicker. Very little would faze him.'

Round 1. South African Grand Prix, Kyalami, 1 March.
Length 2.6 miles (4.2 km).
Race distance 72 laps (190.5 miles/306.7 km).

Completely rebuilt, it was only a very distant relative to the old

Kyalami, last visited by Formula 1 in 1985 when Mansell took pole and won in the Williams Honda. This Kyalami conformed to the prevalent thinking on layouts. It could have been anywhere. Berger reflected that when he said, typically, 'It's a nice track but I don't find it personally very exciting. I would have preferred some more high-speed corners. The fast corners which already exist you can take flat out, anyway. It's difficult to get a good lap.'

Mansell's insight: *'The track is incredibly demanding. The only thing I would like there to be is one long straight, somewhere for overtaking, but even though I am saying that it is fabulous.'*

This followed the exploratory session on the Thursday, and Mansell thundered it. After 8 minutes he was quickest and spent the rest of the session cutting that to reach 1 minute 17 seconds, Berger next in the 1:18s, Senna in the 1:19s. These are, by definition, big margins, but it was too early to regard them as conclusive. Friday would, with hindsight, prove to be that. In the morning free practice:

Mansell	1:16.523
Patrese	1:16.758
Berger	1:17.163
Senna	1:17.344

Qualifying tyres had been banned, which added an unknown dimension. The first qualifying session gave Mansell a vast psychological as well as temporal advantage. He went out early, did a proper warm-up lap then exploded into 1:15.943, eased back to the 1.16s for a couple of laps, backed off to 1:30.361 — gathering himself — then exploded again, 1:15.576. Senna worked himself hard across two runs and needed ten laps to peak at 1:16.815.

Interesting, how the mental and tactical games played themselves out. In second qualifying several cars emerged immediately to try and repeat what Mansell had done on the Friday and have a clear, early run. They returned to the pits like a flock of homing pigeons and, after 11 minutes, Mansell and Senna took it on, Senna straight into the 1:16s.

Mansell's insight: *'I had to abort the first lap and when I came round again Ayrton was on his fast one so I thought I would follow him. When I went into the quick lap I came round at the end of the pit straight, went in really deep and quick and put the car in a nice slide, which seemed OK to start with, then it went away from me. I think it was too quick but there were a lot of people spinning off and an awful lot of dust blowing on the circuit. I was going backwards at 260 kph and I did not enjoy that.'*

Mansell retreated to the spare car and on his last lap exploded again. 1:15.486. Senna reached 1:16.227 but no further.

It was a stunning example of a mature driver with superior machinery

---

Brown says, 'Because of the amount of testing we had done, Nigel was very familiar with what the car felt like and how to get a lap time out of it. At Kyalami there were a couple of quite quick but difficult corners in which there was a lot of time [to be gained] and he was able to go through much quicker than Riccardo. And, watching the TV monitor, they were both quicker than everybody else! The car seemed to suit the way Nigel drove it. It was a car you needed to be aggressive with and there was always something left in the car. If a driver could exploit it, which Nigel was able to do, it would go even faster. He was able to exploit the full potential whereas other people, who didn't have his style of driving, wouldn't have been able to. Yes, he was blindingly quick.

'We did have a few electrical problems in the race car. We did late nights changing everything you could possibly change and we couldn't find it. Ultimately, it turned out to be a wiring loom. We thought we'd found it on the Saturday night but, because we weren't sure, we couldn't race it. That was our attitude and that is the professional attitude towards reliability. So we raced the spare and it was just as good as the race car.'

At the green light, Mansell made a hesitant getaway (relatively — to you and me it would have been Cape Kennedy and an Apollo lift-off) and had the McLarens of Senna and Berger hard behind him. Patrese sliced between the McLarens so that by the first right-hand kink Mansell led from Patrese, Senna and Berger. And that was the story of the race, virtually the story of the season, no less. Senna 'knew right from the start, after such a good getaway by Riccardo, it would be almost impossible to pass him. He went away a bit and although I tried to keep the pressure on he was a little faster than me.

Left *The picture of 1992: Mansell celebrating.*

I was able to maintain a short distance from him and periodically put in a spurt trying to get an opportunity in traffic; or perhaps he would have a technical problem.'

Mansell's insight: *'Ayrton was pressuring Riccardo halfway through the race because I was pushing quite hard and not going away. From then on, it was a question of trying to save a bit of spare time for the traffic, but the traffic was pretty good.'*

Mansell beat Patrese by 24.360 seconds and Senna by 34.675. It was a stunning demonstration of a mature driver wielding superior machinery without undue stress, and controlling a motor race absolutely in each of its component parts. It was stunning at another level, also. Clearly Mansell could do it again and again and again.

Round 2. Mexican Grand Prix, Mexico City, 22 March.
Length 2.7 miles (4.4 km).
Race distance 69 laps (189.5 miles/305.0 km).

Eighteen minutes into first qualifying, Senna's McLaren jud-jud-juddered over the circuit's notorious bumps, snapped out of control and spun on grass. It struck a wall hard enough for Senna to think he'd broken both legs. He hadn't, but he emerged badly shaken and that affected Mansell. 'It was very upsetting because it's not nice to see anybody hurt, least of all the main opposition. To get back in the car and motivate yourself is hard — and I had to push exceedingly hard because Schumacher is driving very well and it was a struggle to get provisional pole.'

Young Schumacher, working his way urgently into his first full season, squeezed 1:17.554 from the Benetton, Mansell bettered that on his 14th lap (1:17.130) and on laps 18 and 20 descended into the 1:16s. It was South Africa again, but here in unlovely, unloved Mexico; during second qualifying Patrese improved, but not quite enough to take pole.

Mansell's insight: *'The team have had to work very hard because I lost my race car from this morning to this afternoon and I used the spare to qualify. When I started to go out I had a computer failure and lost about 15 to 20 minutes, but everything worked well in the end — although the*

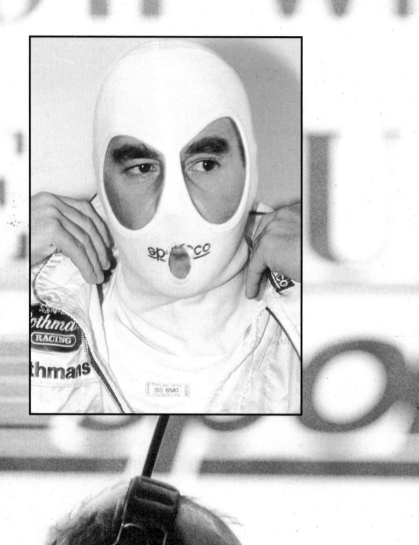

Inset The eyes of 1992: missing nothing.

Main picture The faces of 1992: Frank Williams and Mansell.

engine in the race car is a bit better than the spare. The track is very difficult because so many cars are going off, and when they come back they bring dust. At one point I was going into the fast corner and halfway through my car turned sideways. The only reason I can think is that someone put some dust on a few seconds before me.'

At the green light Mansell moved crisply from Patrese, Senna third, Schumacher hustling Senna. They settled evenly spread, each car dancing the jud-jud-judder until Senna pulled off after 11 laps — clutch or transmission, he wasn't sure.

Mansell's insight: *'The first half of the race was fantastic for me. You might think it was easy but Riccardo knows how much he was pushing and I know how hard I was having to push to stay there. For the first 20 or 30 laps there was virtually nothing between us.'*

Mansell and Patrese constantly swapped fastest laps, but what Patrese couldn't do was hoist himself near enough to attack. After 20 laps the gap stretched to 3.8 seconds and thereafter it stretched further. 'I had a problem and that was Nigel's speed!' Patrese said. 'I had to push very hard and unfortunately my left front tyre had a blister. I was worried that I'd have to stop for tyres so I eased off to bring back the tyres and I managed to finish the race.' Mansell had it by 12.971 seconds from Patrese, Schumacher third.

Round 3. Brazilian Grand Prix, Interlagos, 5 April.
Length 2.6 miles (4.3 km).
Race distance 71 laps (190.7 miles/307.0 km).

McLaren were expected to strike back strongly. They took six cars, among them the new MP4/7A, and 81 personnel. This was serious — and to no avail. Cryptically but accurately, the Williams team distilled first qualifying into this: 'Nigel Mansell and Riccardo Patrese were first and second quickest in their Williams-Renault FW14Bs with times of 1:15.703 and 1:17.591 respectively. Nigel's time came at the beginning of the session on his first set of tyres and he put in four laps that were quicker than anybody else. Riccardo's time was also set on his first set of tyres and he put in four times which were faster than third-placed Michael Schumacher.' Berger was fifth, Senna ninth.

Of the 1:15.703, Mansell, smiling and looking very relaxed, said, 'I think that was one of the best laps I have done in my career. Even I will say it was a good lap. On this circuit there are corners where you haven't time to appreciate and analyse just what you have achieved before you come to the next, and there were a couple on that lap where I just knew I would never go through faster if I went through another hundred times.'

'I made a real duff start — I was pleased I didn't stall!'

On the Saturday Mansell and Senna met at the Bico de Pato corner — Senna moving over on to the racing line for the right-hander, hemming Mansell who swivelled across the grass and thumped the wall. 'I don't hold Ayrton to blame at all. I think it was a mis-communication. I thought that he had pulled over to the right to let me by. We almost touched and the nature of that short straight and the track gave me no opportunity to come back quickly enough. I got into a half-spin and hit the wall. It's as simple as that.' Senna 'only saw that something happened to him when I was out of the corner already. It happened under braking when we were both going slowly. We never touched.'

At the green light, Patrese seized the lead and held it despite a strong inside lunge from Mansell. They crossed the line to complete the opening lap, Patrese, Mansell, Senna, Schumacher. This represented much more than the first lap of the race; it was the first lap of the 1992 season that Mansell had not led. Patrese, grinning afterwards: 'I think the start was OK!' Mansell, also grinning afterwards: 'I made a real duff start, one of my worst ever, and in the end I was pleased I didn't stall.'

For 31 laps Mansell pressed and Patrese resisted, Senna clinging as best he could to lap 17 when the electrics failed. By then Patrese and Mansell had absented themselves into their own race. Mansell pitted for tyres and felt lucky 'because I went in before we hit more traffic'. He remained stationary for 8.54 seconds, Patrese — two laps later — for 9.11 seconds. As Patrese emerged from the pit lane into the downhill twist to the track he glimpsed Mansell passing in the lead. Mansell increased that in a measured way and won by 29.330

seconds, or defeated Patrese by 29.330. Mansell 30 points, Patrese 18, Schumacher 11, Berger 5, Senna 4.

Let us take stock. In South Africa only three drivers finished on the same lap as Mansell and Patrese. They were Senna, Schumacher and Berger. In Mexico, only Schumacher and Berger. In Brazil, nobody. There had been 16 sessions apart from the races: Mansell quickest in 14, Patrese the other two. Mansell had three pole positions from three, three wins from three and one fastest lap (Berger and Patrese the other two). Of the 212 race laps, Mansell led 180, Patrese the other 32. We had come face to face with something almost total.

Some critics sought to diminish this by insisting that the Williams car/engine was so superior to the others that any of a dozen drivers would have won races in it. You can always insist that. A better line of argument is to compare the two team-mates who did have the car. Thus far Mansell had come near to destroying Patrese. The late James Hunt, trenchant but truthful, even lambasted Patrese on the BBC during Kyalami with the message 'Time to go home, Riccardo,

Victory in South Africa and a thumbs up.

and not come back'. It provoked a minor furore but contained a pertinent question. Given the same car/engine, what was Patrese up to?

The simple answer might be that he wasn't as good as Mansell. Patrese was a genuinely nice man who, after a tempestuous start to his career, had settled down into benign middle age (in Formula 1 terms), didn't cause trouble but didn't win many races (five in 15 years) either. If Patrese can be taken as typical of middle- to upper-ranking drivers, it leaves precious few who might have contained Mansell. Senna? Yes. Berger? Possibly. Schumacher? Maybe. Moreover, 1992 was the first time Mansell had a machine that could only be beaten by his team-mate across the compass of a season, and on the evidence thus far it seemed desperately unlikely. It left Nigel Mansell very alone, very isolated. He wanted the World Championship badly and, a month into the campaign, only a single person remained who could beat him to it.

Himself.

Round 4. Spanish Grand Prix, Barcelona, 3 May.
Length 2.9 miles (4.7 km).
Race distance 65 laps (191.7 miles/308.5 km).

Before this, Mansell gave an extensive interview to the British magazine *Motoring News*, and I reproduce the kernel of it because here is a man holding his balance. *Motoring News* began with a couple of statements and moulded them into a question.

You have won three out of three races so far and started from pole each time. Never before has a team dominated the start of a Formula 1 season in this way. What do you think the reasons are for your superiority?

'It's very difficult to say. There's never one single reason why one wins. I would say more a combination of reasons. It's like a chain. If one of the links is weak the chain will break. Before, there were four factors necessary for success: the chassis, the engine, the tyres and the driver. Today there is one other factor: fuel. This year, Williams has worked a lot, Renault has worked a lot, Elf has worked a lot and Damon Hill, our test driver, has worked a lot on behalf of Riccardo and myself. When you put all that together you've a fantastic team.

Furthermore, the foundations of the team are deep and sound. I've spent a total of six years with Williams and won 21 Grands Prix with it. I know everyone there. I can speak openly with Frank, tell him things which aren't necessarily nice to hear without that affecting the confidence we have in one another. He knows he can tell me anything, too. It takes time to reach that degree of mutual confidence. Today I feel stronger than ever before. I have never been in better physical shape. I don't think I have ever loved being a racing driver so much.'

At Barcelona in the Friday free practice Mansell did a 1:19, Patrese next on 1:20.187, Schumacher third, Senna fourth. In first qualifying Mansell did 1:20.190, Schumacher next (1:21.195), Senna third (1:21.209), Patrese fourth (1:21.534). It rained on the Saturday, leaving the Friday time undisturbed. It rained on the Sunday, too, the race officially declared wet.

At the green light Mansell dug the power and occupied mid-track with Patrese behind: the familiar story. Mansell stretched from Patrese, a crocodile of cars in pursuit, but the stretching intensifying instant by instant. Patrese went off on lap 20. Schumacher cut the gap to Mansell who responded, settling the race provided Mansell didn't slide off. The rain fell harder into the gathering murk, tyres churned standing water and, to demonstrate the perils, Senna wobbled, recovered, spun, recovered, spun, didn't recover ('the car was aquaplaning everywhere'). Mansell beat Schumacher by 23.914 seconds.

Mansell's insight: *'I think it was one of the hardest races of my career. I can't remember having to drive so hard for so long. I was fighting just to stay on the circuit. I set the car up with a compromise in case it dried out, so we suffered a little bit. However, any driver will tell you that in these conditions the set-up will not be perfect.'*

'Two-thirds of the way through,' Brown says, 'Nigel was beginning to struggle. Schumacher was taking streets out of him and I remember Nigel saying after the race he thought he was in trouble. "This is going to be a problem, the guy is going to catch me." We were all thinking there would be a fight near the end. It rained harder and harder. Nigel discovered that by taking a different line round all the corners he suddenly picked up a lot of grip. He went round experimenting in a search for grip, thinking 'if I can't do something,

Schumacher will be on me'. That was it, Nigel was away.' Mansell 40 points, Patrese 18, Schumacher 17, Berger 8, Alesi 7, Senna 4.

Round 5. San Marino Grand Prix, Imola, 17 May.
Length 3.1 miles (5.0 km).
Race distance 60 laps (187.9 miles/302.4 km).

Senna won the first four races of 1991 and Mansell had equalled that, of course. Five-in-a-row beckoned, and the portents were immediately good, Mansell quickest in both Friday sessions climaxing with 1:21.842 in first qualifying — the fastest ever lap of Imola. 'I used every bit of the track and maybe more. I was eleven-tenths on some corners, if you want to put it like that.' On the Saturday, Mansell couldn't improve although Patrese did, but not by enough (1:22.895); and that was five poles in a row.

At the green light Mansell shed Patrese, Senna third but falling from them even on this opening lap. After a mere nine laps Mansell lay some 17 seconds ahead of Senna, even though Senna had 'some sort of cramp in my shoulders caused by the vibration of the car and

The rush to turn one in Mexico.

the tension involved in keeping it on the road.' By race's end only Senna and Brundle were on the same lap as Mansell and Patrese.

Mansell's insight: *'I wanted to run my own race because I knew my tyres were marginal. I think without my training during the winter I would have been in the same situation as Senna. It was a tough race from the physical point of view because I had cramp and muscle spasms down my right leg.'*

Mansell 50 points, Patrese 24, Schumacher 17, Senna 8, Berger 8, Alesi 7; and the five-in-a-row. Could Mansell win all 16? It seemed entirely possible, but that particular question would be answered two weeks later by, of all things, a naughty wheel nut. Or, as Brown says, 'If you've won the first five races you're in pretty reasonable shape, aren't you? Then Monaco, which we quite famously failed to win . . .'

Round 6. Monaco Grand Prix, Monte Carlo, 31 May.
Length 2.0 miles (3.3 km).
Race distance 78 laps (161.3 miles/259.5 km).

Here, in theory and at last, a circuit presented itself to Ayrton Senna where his forbidding logic, precision and judgement might allow him to negate the Mansell advantage. If Senna wrested pole he'd be dauntingly awkward to overtake however much faster the Williams might be; and Senna had taken pole in 1988, 1989, 1990 and 1991.

First qualifying was like touching an exposed electrical cable, Mansell on provisional pole from Senna (1:20.714 against 1:21.467), Patrese third (1:22.309).

Mansell's insight: *'I tried to respond to Ayrton's time on my worn set of tyres and the best I could do was 1:21.9, then fortunately I went out and got almost a clear lap on a fresh set. I had a "moment". It's a bit of a problem when you arrive at the chicane backwards heading into the sea wall. I dropped the clutch, thought the impact is going to happen any minute then the car went sideways, slowed down, accelerated. I spun through 360 degrees and carried on going the way I was. I was very lucky not to hit the wall.'*

Second qualifying remained electric, Patrese now firmly into the equation, too. Mansell went out after 12 minutes and worked down to 1:20.890 despite being hampered by a slower car at the very end of the lap. He eased off for a couple of laps, tried again and found a fraction within the fractions. 1:20.774. Inside 20 minutes Patrese responded with 1:20.847, composed himself, wound up and up. 1:20.560. Mansell, soon out again, wound up and up. 1:20.369. Senna limped to the pits after a spin at Mirabeau and a clout of the armco. 'It was going to be a good lap but I drove over the limit to try and make up the time somehow,' Senna said. Out came Patrese again, wound up and up. 1:20.368.

It gave Patrese pole by one thousandth of a second. Mansell wasn't having any of that. He'd do some more winding. 'I must confess that I flat spotted my second set of tyres [locked wheels under braking, skimming a slice of rubber off]. I took a big chunk out of the front. I went back on to my first set and I didn't think there was any way I was going to do it. I then thought I'd coast round and try to feel where the grip was, because sometimes it was changing from lap to lap. I hung it out on about three corners and knew if I was going to hit the barriers I was going to hit them because I wanted pole position. It was just phenomenal — even for me — being in the car!' 1:19.495.

'Nigel was off on to a completely different planet in the race'

At the green light, Mansell swivelled to mid-track, making the pressure-point of Ste Devote corner — where places can be lost and won — safe for him. From the second row of the grid Senna lunged inside, used the kerbing and took second place. 'I went for it at the last moment,' Senna revealed, 'so as not to give Riccardo any indication — because otherwise he would have closed the door, of course. I got into second place that way but the problem was to stop the car before Mansell turned in, because I was coming so quickly I thought he might not have seen me. If Riccardo had been ahead of me out of the corner, I doubt I would ever have got past him.'

Senna accepted soon enough that even he could not stay with Mansell. 'No way I could keep up. Impossible, with the superiority of his car. I tried to go hard enough to be in a position to benefit if anything happened to Mansell, but still try to conserve my tyres, particularly on full tanks in the early laps.' Monaco is full of danger

Main picture *Victory in Brazil* (Camel).

Inset *The podium in Brazil, everyone delighted.* (Camel).

and uncertainty, as such a narrow place must be in a Formula 1 car, but Senna applied his forbidding logic to this seemingly insoluble problem. 'Already in the early race I was planning for the late race.'

Patrese hustled Senna but Senna eased away. By then Mansell was in his own race. Here and there he'd tick off fastest laps — 18, 22, 39, 60. By then Senna lay 28 seconds behind, watching and waiting as they moved into the late race. On lap 71, suddenly and without warning, Mansell toured down the incline from the tunnel. 'Coming through the tunnel I almost lost it and the back end went down. I felt immediately that I had a puncture. The problem was that I was halfway from the pits and I had to drive slowly to get there. I had a longer pit stop than normal and as I came out of the pits I saw Ayrton go by and I knew that the race was probably lost.'

Brown says, 'Nigel was off on to a completely different planet in the race and quite near the end he came on the radio saying, "I've got a puncture". I thought, bloody hell, this is not what we need. He came in and we changed the wheel but we had a look round the tyre as he went out of the pit and he didn't have a puncture.' The wheel nut had come loose. Senna led by 5.1 seconds on lap 72.

	Mansell	Senna
Lap 72	1:27.523	1:24.212
Lap 73	1:22.974	1:23.764

That was fastest lap of the race. On the start-finish straight going into the lap, Mansell had taken Michele Alboreto (Footwork) and now had only Erik Comas (Ligier) between himself and Senna. Mansell caught and scythed past Comas at the Mirabeau hard-right as if a great, gathering momentum held him. The gap: 5.159.

Lap 74	1:21.598	1:24.007

Mansell flung the Williams at Casino Square and it twitched visibly under the momentum. After lap 74 he'd butchered the gap to 1.960. Next lap, only four to go, a backmarker — JJ Lehto (Dallara) — loomed helplessly ahead of Senna. At the chicane after the tunnel, Lehto couldn't help holding Senna up and the momentum brought Mansell full to Senna. On the rush to Tabac, Senna darted out and went by Lehto, Mansell darted out and went by Lehto. They crossed the line nose-to-tail, three laps to go.

Up the hill to Casino, Mansell feinted left, nosed right. Senna held the racing line rigidly. At the chicane Senna forced enough power to stop Mansell making any move — Senna must have remembered the race the year before when Mansell had done precisely this to Prost, goading the Williams, pressing it into the mouth of the chicane and forcing Prost to crash or concede. Towards Tabac, Mansell feinted left but still Senna filled the circuit.

Two laps to go and Mansell searched for an opening, any opening, any half-chance, anything. Senna seemed neat and precise and that was all he had to be, just follow that invisible thread called the racing line, keep filling the narrowness of the circuit. Inside the cockpit, Senna's world seemed anything but neat and precise. 'For the last five or six laps I had nothing left to give. My tyres were finished and I had no grip. And I was tired. It was hell to push at that point. I knew Mansell would try everything and all I could do was try to stay on the road and in the right place. It was like a drag race on the straights, wheelspin in third and fourth gears.'

> *'If you've won the first five races, not winning the sixth is like not finishing in comparison'*

Mansell darted and probed and they crossed the line into the last lap. Senna milked out enough to protect himself at Mirabeau and through the tunnel to the chicane, and past the swimming pool, and through the bent spoon of Rascasse which brings the cars on to the start-finish straight and the line. Rascasse is so tight, and the car ahead has such an advantage getting on the power first to exit it, that the race is settled. Senna's winning margin — 0.215 — would have been a hold-your-breath finish anywhere but here. Mansell could do nothing except follow. 'Ayrton's car was just too wide to get past, although he was perfectly entitled to do what he did to defend his position. We were both driving way over the limit for the last few laps.'

'Nigel was philosophical,' Brown says, 'obviously disappointed because he wanted to win so much and he'd tried very, very hard to do that. His eyeballs were like dinner plates after the race, but he said, "Well, OK, as long as we can fix it we'll be all right for the next

Main picture *The team-mate, Riccardo Patrese.*

Inset *Patrese, animated, with Williams designer Patrick Head.*

race", and of course it's all more points towards the Championship. However, if you've won the first five, not winning the sixth is like not finishing in comparison — but you still take the points . . .'

The week after, Williams confirmed that it had been a loose wheel nut. Designer Patrick Head said, 'We have gone to tremendous lengths to avoid it happening again [a similar problem had hobbled Mansell in Hungary in 1987, and 1991 at Estoril]. In all the testing and racing we have done since, there has been absolutely no indication of such a problem, and Riccardo's car was perfectly OK. The wheels had all been fully and properly torqued. It was just a problem on that particular rear wheel. Nigel did exactly the right thing coming in. If he hadn't, he might well have ended up as a three-wheeler out there on the circuit.' Mansell 56 points, Patrese 28, Schumacher 20, Senna 18, Berger 8, Alesi 7. Hereabouts, rumours began to circulate that Alain Prost would be joining Mansell at Williams in 1993. These rumours were initially propounded by Hunt on the BBC, and Mansell, who needed peace of mind, called the speculation 'unprofessional'.

Round 7. Canadian Grand Prix, Montreal, 14 June.
Length 2.7 miles (4.4 km).
Race distance 69 laps (189.9 miles/305.6 km).

Senna took provisional pole, the first time Mansell hadn't (Patrese second, Mansell fourth). It rained before second qualifying and, although the track dried, only Mansell of the top four could improve, his 1:19.948 worth third overall.

Mansell compared the circuit to Monaco because overtaking is notoriously tricky here, too. On the Ile Notre Dame, pole can bestow similar riches to Monaco. Senna knew that and said so; and added with his own particular candour that, if he — Senna — failed to reach the first corner first, Mansell would be gone into the clear blue yonder and the next time they'd see each other would be on the podium. It made the pressure point the same as Ste Devote.

At the green light Mansell tried to bore between Patrese and Senna and did get past Patrese, but by the next corner, a hard left, Senna led decisively. For 14 laps the order remained passive. Clearly Mansell could go quicker than Senna but — again like Monaco —

he must get past to prove that. Gaps, statistics and lap times were irrelevant. A seven-car crocodile observed decorum while Senna followed the racing line, which, given his precision and concentration, he could do indefinitely; but everybody knew, absolutely knew, that Nigel Ernest James Mansell would not follow Ayrton Senna da Silva tamely and obediently for the remaining 55 laps of the Canadian Grand Prix.

Completing lap 15 they reached towards the chicane that would feed them to the start-finish straight. It might be an overtaking place and it might not, this tight little right-left chicane. Mansell tried down the inside but the track was dirty there. Berger, reluctantly commenting afterwards, suggested that Senna made his car 'quite wide'. The hard-right speared at them. Mansell couldn't take the corner and went across Senna, went on over the sand and grass at the far side of the chicane. The Williams bounced-bounded and lost its nose cone, bounced-bounded bisecting the chicane and continued, mauled, until it regained the circuit on the start-finish straight, spinning. It came to rest there, its broken snout peering mutedly at the oncoming traffic.

The rain in Spain didn't stop Mansell, by now masterful.

Mansell sat immobile in the cockpit, Senna safely by, Patrese safely by — but Patrese said that 'when Nigel went off he came across in front of me and I didn't know where he was landing, unfortunately. I had to lift and Berger got by.' Mansell sat until the cars came round to complete lap 16. As Senna passed, Mansell was in the process of levering himself out. With his left hand he made a stabbing gesture of accusation and anger towards Senna. Several marshals helped Mansell to the pit lane wall and hoisted him over it. He limped. He took his helmet off and vented his rage on a roving television reporter (who, to be fair to Mansell, asked a grotesque question. 'Are you on your way to the Media Centre to make a statement?'). He vented his rage to Ron Dennis, his future employer. He proceeded to the Steward's Office where, although he did not lodge an official protest, he made his feelings known. The Stewards were reported to be less than sympathetic.

'Nigel appeared, sitting in the middle of the circuit, the rest streaming around him'

Paradoxically Brown, who'd been on the pit lane wall, 'didn't see the incident until I got back to the hotel because there was a hoarding in the way. I saw a big cloud of sand, Nigel appeared sitting in the middle of the circuit, the rest of them streaming round him, and he was waving his arms trying to get the race stopped, I think. That was that. Afterwards he was very upset and he thought Ayrton had moved over on him. When I saw it, I wasn't really sure. When the driver is in the car racing, all he needs is half an impression something is happening and he has to make his decision. To Nigel it may have been like that. I was never really sure.

'Ayrton had got into the lead and was holding everybody up. Typical Montreal. You can't overtake. I think Nigel was beginning to think "if I don't get round him, we're going to be in trouble" — whereas Ayrton's performance was more Ayrton's own performance than the car's. Had Nigel waited a bit longer he may have found an easier opportunity. He wasn't that sort of bloke. He found it difficult to sit behind someone, but it was not a matter of lack of self-control because Nigel was a highly disciplined driver. On the radio he was very disciplined, always thinking about all the aspects of the race, not simply "who am I going to overtake next?". He'd consider the race as the whole length of the race, and right from the beginning he'd try and plot his way through it, like a mature man — which is what made him so good, of course.'

Senna dropped out after 37 laps — electrics — and said, 'My opinion of Nigel's retirement is that he realised he couldn't brake in time for the corner, so he lined the car up with the middle of the kerb and hoped to clear it, but he hit it with such force that he appeared to land on the car's nose.'

Mansell offered crisp words. 'I've always been told that if you can't say something good about somebody, it's best to say nothing at all. That is all I have to say.' Mansell 56 points, Patrese 28, Schumacher 26, Senna and Berger 18, Alesi 11.

The week after Montreal, Frank Williams denied the rumours that the team had signed Prost — evidently these rumours had upset Mansell in Canada. 'We have absolutely no comment to make about any discussions,' Williams said, as he would and as he usually does. 'Obviously we are talking to everyone, but it is not appropriate to make any comment at the moment.' Whatever it was, it wasn't good news for nice Riccardo Patrese.

Round 8. French Grand Prix, Magny-Cours, 5 July.
Length 2.6 miles (4.2 km).
Race distance 69 laps (182.2 miles/293.2 km).

The natural order was restored in first qualifying: Mansell 1.15.047, Patrese 1:15.551, Senna 1:16.892, Berger 1:16.944. Mansell put together eight laps of 1.15s and Patrese three. In direct comparison, Senna and Berger were able to reach the 1:16s only once. Second qualifying confirmed the order.

A rain-racked race, and at the green light Patrese led immediately from Mansell. Schumacher launched a virile attempt to take Senna at the hairpin and rammed him off and out. Senna stood beyond the barrier, helmet clasped behind his back, watching the defence of his championship ebbing; but from heavy cloud the rain began. Mansell had been attacking Patrese, of course. 'At the start Riccardo drove brilliantly and got a great start and we had a lot of fun.' Then the red flags came out, the race stopped because of the weather. Patrese held a 0.935 'lead' when the race, now over an aggregate of two legs, resumed. Patrese repeated his first start but Mansell attacked again and slotted inside at the Adelaide hairpin. Patrese responded — Mansell drifting wide — and retook him. Crossing the start-finish line, however, Patrese raised an arm and signalled Mansell through. Patrese did this with something of a flourish as if he wanted the world to see and understand what he was doing. Afterwards Patrese wouldn't confirm that the team had ordered him to do this.

Brown adds intriguingly, 'No, I don't think there were team orders. I think Riccardo moved over and let him by because Nigel would have been at him all the way through the race and honestly I don't think Riccardo wanted Nigel sat on his tail for the entire duration, which Nigel would certainly have done. It was so obvious what was going to happen. From the outset of the season, Nigel was out there to prove that he was quicker than Riccardo — because the first thing you do is stamp on your team-mate. Then everything goes your way and you get on and beat everybody else.' Mansell won by

Imola, and his fifth straight win.

46.447 seconds. Mansell 66, Patrese 34, Schumacher 26, Senna and Berger 18, Alesi 11.

The background became as murky as the weather. Patrese had been seen in discussion with Benetton's commercial director, Flavio Briatore. More rumours, which Frank Williams denied, insinuated that Patrese had been told he'd been fired. The Prost-for-Williams rumours intensified, making Mansell defensive. He had not yet re-signed for 1993. 'We are getting closer to an agreement,' Mansell said, 'but I want to firm up who the other driver is going to be. Until I know, I'm not prepared to commit myself to anything.'

Round 9. British Grand Prix, Silverstone, 12 July.
Length 3.2 miles (5.2 km).
Race distance 59 laps (191.5 miles/308.3 km).

Something of a mystery endures about the final moments of the Sunday at Silverstone. We know what happened but not really why. My own feeling is that a conjunction of factors came together and each fed the other so voraciously that something gave way. Sanity.

Maybe, with hindsight, it had been building since 1986 when Mansell won the British Grand Prix at Brands Hatch after a monumental struggle with his Williams team-mate Nelson Piquet. Mansell repeated this at Silverstone in 1987, beating Piquet by 1.918 seconds. Mansell finished second to Senna in 1988, when the race moved permanently to Silverstone. In 1989 Mansell, now Ferrari, finished second to Prost (Marlboro McLaren). In 1990 Mansell took pole, led the race twice, set fastest lap but dropped out when the gearbox failed. He then announced his retirement. Lured back by Frank Williams, he won decisively in 1991 from Berger. Cumulatively from 1986 Mansell created the communion with his own people, each year making it more intimate, more profound. One part of the mystery is: who were those people?

The thousands at Silverstone were almost completely British (one might narrow that to English) and they had come to commune with Our Nige who was as English as they. He belonged to Mother England. He constantly expressed his patriotism, didn't speak another language, didn't evidently like foreign food and lived in the Isle of Man, not Monaco. In many important ways, he was just like

Left *Monaco, the pit stop and the cruel race.*

the thousands and they were just like him.

Success attracts. A winning football team finds its gates rise significantly, for example. Beyond question Mansell's success increased the gate at Silverstone by a massive factor; the year after, when he'd gone, it fell by more than half. Success attracts in a more subtle fashion, too. It bestows reflected importance on those who witnessed it *because I was there*. Maybe that alone made Silverstone the place to be that weekend, and afterwards the place to tell your mates you'd been. Maybe many among the thousands knew nothing of motor racing, its ways and its etiquettes, nor cared.

On the Friday, normally genteel, the atmosphere resembled a race day, sharp and hard. Mansell moved like rolling thunder. In first qualifying, with the chance of rain lurking, most runners emerged promptly to lock up a safe time. Mansell covered five laps, worked into 1:20.762, paused for breath, worked on down into 1:20.503. It would have been, as it happened, good enough for provisional pole. On Mansell's second run he worked into the 1:19s three times, climaxing at 1:19.161. (Senna's second run brought a 1:21.706, Patrese 1:20.884). With 4 minutes remaining Mansell could have wandered to the motorhome at his leisure, had a shower and read the paper. He decided to go out again 'for the sake of the crowd'. He reasoned that another 1:19 might be possible and they'd like to witness that. Here was a man at the height of his powers with a car at the height of its powers and an awesome engine propelling both of them. Now we had a conjunction of willpowers: Mansell willing himself to something absolutely exceptional and the thousands willing him to it.

How to describe a single lap, make the differences between it and so many other laps? At moments, this one seemed almost primitive in its thrust and strength, almost brutal in the manner of its delivery; a man violently arm-wrestling 3.247 miles of tarmacadam into submission. The timing devices froze at 1:18.965 as he crossed the line, Silverstone lost to wild tumult. 'It was so quick I can't imagine going any quicker. This is the meanest and most physical circuit in the world and I really gave it everything. I am aching all over — including my teeth. There is so much G force on this track. You have to

Main picture *The communion, Silverstone.*

Inset *The line, Silverstone, and total victory over Patrese.*

commit. I am able to commit in my race car and I am able to do something which I feel is special at Silverstone.'

Brown remembers that 'Silverstone was good fun, we thoroughly enjoyed Silverstone. Nigel was unbelievably quick, particularly in qualifying. The 1:18 was a hell of a lap and it wasn't necessary for him to do it. He was already on pole. It was like "Come on David, let's have another go", and I thought "All right, OK, off you go", and we put the tyres on and off he did go. Because he was [invariably] quickest the television cameras would cover him, so we had the TV pictures. He was really quick through Copse and Becketts, which is where he got most of his time from. The lap was astonishing. We get three split times; we looked and after the first one I thought, "Hang on, this looks quick, this does", and we peered at the TV harder. When it was over everybody was in the mood of "See that, our driver's just done that!" It was so memorable, the guy who did all the data recording presented Nigel with a framed copy of the data from that lap.'

The session forged the tone for the weekend, no matter that it rained for second qualifying. The crowd on the Sunday would be 120,000, every road and lane feeding the circuit blocked for many a mile. By mid-morning Silverstone teemed. Inevitably Mansell quickened the tone during morning warm-up: 1:24.968, then Patrese 1:25.738, then Schumacher 1:26.259.

At the green light Mansell churned a little wheelspin, enough to let Patrese lead into Copse, but Mansell uncoiled like a taut spring and by Becketts drew level, went through. 'Riccardo made a fantastic start and then we were going side by side, just having a nice Sunday afternoon drive up to Becketts, and then I managed to get the slingshot.'

The British Grand Prix as a motor race (in the sense of finding out who'd win) lasted those few seconds. From the exit of Becketts, Mansell moved further into his own race than he had ever been before. He led lap one by 3.2 seconds and increased that to over 20 seconds by lap ten. On lap four, and with virtually full tanks, he destroyed the track record with 1:26.327. The year before he'd set it at 1:26.379. Eleven times he hammered out fastest lap. Nigel Mansell

Right *Victory in Germany, the last step before the Championship.*

made the British Grand Prix a solo run, beating Patrese by 39.094 seconds and reducing the record to 1:22.539 — a genuinely astonishing gain of nearly 4 seconds.

As Mansell emerged from Luffield, the final corner before the start-finish straight and victory, a significant section of the crowd in the grandstands rushed the wire perimeter fence. Mansell crossed the line, fist out waving, and, behind him, a spectator *ran across the track*. Television caught that: a spectre of a figure in a yellow day-glo hat, a Union Jack wrapped around his jeans. Brown remembers that 'Patrick Head leapt on to the radio and said to Nigel, "There are people on the circuit!"' By Copse corner, a dozen, two dozen, three dozen spectators burst on to the track from the infield, arms outstretched to embrace Their Nige.

Fifteen cars still travelled at racing speed.

A tide of spectators poured through the fence beside the finish line

At Copse, Mansell swivelled the car from the on-rush, but by now a tide of spectators poured through the fence. As Patrese came by they flooded like a ragged army along the grass beside the finishing line. As Berger finished, engine blown, hundreds packed the grass. If Berger had dropped oil and spun . . .

During the slowing-down lap, Mansell was completely engulfed, lost from sight. Helplessly he ran over somebody's foot. Many of those who engulfed him brandished their fists in a football gesture when a team scores: tribal, aggressive. This was not the most alarming part. Large numbers ran on to the circuit while the race was still going on. Perhaps they did not grasp even such fundamentals as that a race does not cease when the winner crosses the line, that others behind are keeping a wary eye open to steal a place or two — as Schumacher did when Berger's engine went. Probably they didn't care about the others. Their Nige was complete unto himself, the others irrelevant; not just bit-part players, but nothing. The tribe had come to claim their inheritance and did not understand what it was when they held it.

(Interestingly, however, Brown says that 'although the car got mobbed around Abbey, it was complete afterwards. If it had stopped in other countries, it would have been in bits; but nothing was missing except a bit of broken bodywork, because somebody had stood on it, I think.')

Every driver you spoke to expressed horror and consternation. Patrese looked livid, Brundle visibly shaken. He was man enough to confess that he'd been frightened. Mansell might have been in a dilemma but evidently wasn't. 'I'm not going to knock them [his supporters]. In a way I would like to compliment them. I think that today has been the most wonderful day for the sport in the history of Formula 1 at Silverstone. I would like to dedicate this historic win to all the fans.' Herein lay the paradox of Mansell, and it is a delicate matter liable to several interpretations. He must have known how close the invasion could have come to slaughter, but he — he alone — had been a catalyst for bringing 120,000 people to a circuit for communion. How many men have known such moments? Not many. How many men could cope with such moments? Not many. How many men could resist being worshipped by a significant proportion of the 120,000 to the point where they risked presenting themselves as sacrifices before moving racing cars?

Something changed at Silverstone, a bastion fell and amidst it stood a man who understood worship, because its gestures and sounds echoed through him, and seemed overwhelmed by it. The consequences were frightening — possibly blood on the floor, next of kin informed by the police and what is the government doing about this? It all created a bizarre by-product. When Mansell returned to Formula 1 in 1995 — and before the season began — Silverstone issued a statement dated 24 February headed:

1995 BRITISH GRAND PRIX CROWD LIMIT
'Advance ticket sales for the 1995 British Grand Prix on 16 July are going at such a rate that, in an unprecedented move, Silverstone Circuit will restrict the number of spectators to 90,000 each day to avoid the overcrowding suffered by spectators in 1992, when 120,000 people packed into the Northamptonshire facility on Grand Prix Sunday. There will be no tickets available at the gates on the Sunday, although spectators will still be able to purchase entry on the gate for the Friday and Saturday.

"'Bookings are up by a massive 300%. We have as many people booked now as we had by mid-June last year,' commented Denys Rohan, Silverstone's Chief Executive. "It looks as though we are heading for an outstanding event. With so many British drivers in competitive cars, interest in Grand Prix racing in the UK has never been higher. We want to ensure that every one of our spectators is comfortable, can see the track and will want to return in 1996," he continued, "although all but 2,000 seats from the total of 29,000 are sold for Grand Prix Sunday."'

Curious. It did not mention Mansell. With him — whether spectators felt comfortable or not — you had the 120,000, without him a third of that; and, deep into May 1995 and the announcement, who knew how many would still go to Silverstone?

A quiet summer's evening, however, the beatitude of 12 July 1992, all the roads blocked again as the gathering struggled to disperse. Mansell 76 points, Patrese 40, Schumacher 29, Berger 20, Senna 18, Brundle 13. The topic had become where and when the Championship would fall to Mansell, and Senna's record of eight wins in a season, set in 1988, was immediately vulnerable.

Round 10. German Grand Prix, Hockenheim, 26 July.
Length 4.2 miles (6.8 km).
Race distance 45 laps (190.5 miles/306.6 km).

Rumours persisted that Patrese would be leaving for 1993, to be replaced by Prost, who was quoted as saying, 'I hope we can make a decision in the next two weeks'. Mansell, meanwhile, took pole.

At the green light Patrese made the better start, but Mansell powered by into the first chicane. Mansell pitted unexpectedly early for tyres on lap 14. 'Because of its long straights, you don't want any problems with tyres at a place like Hockenheim,' Brown says. 'What Nigel didn't know, and what we did know, was that someone ahead of him [a backmarker] had gone off at the entrance to the Stadium section and thrown sand on to the circuit. When Nigel ran over it — well, if a car starts to go sideways he'd be saying to himself, "Don't think much of this, got a puncture, got to go in". The good thing was he had a lead.'

Senna moved into second place behind Patrese. Urgently Mansell

The Hungaroring, Mansell stalking the McLarens.

caught Senna, but Senna held him; and in his urgency Mansell went off at the new chicane before the Ostkurve, the Williams chewing a traffic cone, scampering across dust and rejoining. After that Mansell caught Senna very, very quickly and swept imperiously by. Patrese pitted for tyres on lap 19 and Mansell beat Senna by 4¹/₂ seconds.

'At the start the car jumped from first gear to third. I thought it was better to leave it in third rather than try to get second that it had already missed. Needless to say I was in second place into the first corner, but Riccardo went in a bit deep and I managed to get a really good tow down the straight and get the lead at the first chicane. When I pitted I was pretty convinced I had a puncture and, rather than second guess it and go for another lap, I went into the pits for a new set. Obviously it was too early but I had no choice and, in the end, I just had to try and conserve my tyres. I refuse even to talk about the championship. We shall just have to wait for Hungary.'

Brown points out that Senna drove the whole race on one set of tyres and 'he was going like crazy at the end. It was a very good drive from Ayrton. Nigel's tyres were blistered to hell. The first set had had a couple of blisters but the second set were blistered all over the place. After the race people were saying McLaren were closing the gap to us because Ayrton had been so close to Riccardo before Riccardo went off near the end, but we said, "Hang on, hang on, our other driver won the race!"' Mansell 86 points, Patrese 40, Schumacher 33, Senna 24, Berger 20, Brundle 16.

Round 11. Hungarian Grand Prix, Hungaroring, 16 August.
Length 2.4 miles (3.9 km).
Race distance 77 laps (189.8 miles/305.5 km).

His time had come. All else — 12 years waiting, thrice thwarted — was memory. If he won here, he won the championship. If he finished second to anybody but Patrese he won the championship. If he failed to do that, and Patrese won the race and kept on winning the races — Belgium, Italy, Portugal, Japan and Australia — he needed no more than a third place somewhere, anywhere. Statistics had favoured him before, at Adelaide in 1986, but not on this scale. It should have been a celebration, a consummation

At the public level, Mansell approached the summit by keeping a steady, knowing eye through the two days of qualifying, and no histri-onics. Murray Walker of the BBC, who'd known, watched and inter-viewed Mansell throughout his Formula 1 career, says that 'over the weekend he was probably in a bit of a state inside but he was very contained — that's the word I would use. Nigel is incredibly profes-sional. He was doing a Nigel Mansell videotape and on race morning he drove into the circuit and stopped. He was in a Range Rover or a vehicle like that. [Rather than be irritated] he addressed the camera saying, "Well, this is the day I can win the Championship" and so forth.'

Brown reinforces the impression. 'Nigel was in good shape, wasn't at all uptight because it was only just over half way through the season, for goodness sake, and so there would be plenty of further opportunities. At some stage he said to me, "Well, let's just do our normal job and if we don't win it here we'll win it at the next race. There's no point in getting uptight about it." How was I? I was fine

The return in 1995 – to McLaren.

The return – and everybody wanted to know all about it (ICN U.K. Bureau).

Expectations were high because he'd won the World Championship in 1992.

Left *Then he'd added the IndyCar Championship in 1993 (Allsport).*

He always did like a bit of football. This is Spain 1991.

The 1992 Championship started with a crushing win in South Africa.

The podium, Spain.

Monaco was cruel, and exhausting.

Hungary and 'hey, we've done it!' Mansell has the Championship at last.

Wife Rosanne looks pleased, too.

Left *The communion at Silverstone.*

Not all 1992 was smooth, though. He crashed at the chicane in Canada trying to overtake Ayrton Senna (Associated Press).

Contemplating IndyCar racing, 1993.

The communion, transferred to Phoenix.

At Phoenix Mansell discovers that oval racing can be starkly dangerous (Allsport).

The aftermath of the crash. It happened in practice.

The busiest race in the world, the Indianapolis 500, can also be lonely (Allsport).

In action at Elkhart Lake, where he finished second (Allsport).

The Championship clincher, 1993 (Allsport).

What a team: Carl Haas, Mansell, Paul Newman (Allsport).

And a kiss for Rosanne (Allsport).

In late 1993 Mansell competed in a Touring Car race at Donington and this is what a vast crowd saw (Raymonds).

Guesting for the Williams team, he won the 1994 Australian Grand Prix.

Imola 1995, and much to ponder.

The picture that captures it all. The raised arm means 'I'm in trouble'.

because we'd chat all the time and as long as Nigel was happy and confident then I was.'

At the private level, Mansell, Prost and Senna moved into a subtle but hardly sophisticated contractual poker game for Williams drives in 1993. Mansell tried to protect the cards he held, Prost kept his deftly out of sight and Senna would suddenly show his hand.

Frank Williams travelled to Hungary 'optimistic' that a deal with Mansell could be done, however much Prost loomed as Mansell's potential partner. Williams subsequently explored his thinking. 'The most important thing a Grand Prix team needs is an engine supplier — an engine manufacturer — as your partner. Therefore, in order to keep Renault on-side with Williams, we felt it would be useful, if not invaluable, to have Alain Prost as a team member.'

Mansell, titular World Champion, had reason to feel he'd carved an extremely strong negotiating position. When Frank Williams lured him from 'retirement' in 1991, Mansell had also been in an extremely strong negotiating position and secured virtually everything he'd demanded. That included the benefits of undisputed Number 1 status over Patrese, which Patrese accepted. It bestowed on Mansell what he likes to call a 'comfort zone'. Prost was scarcely likely to accept being Number 2 and, anyway, Prost wanted a 'comfort zone' of his own. He might share it with Mansell but he certainly wouldn't share it with Ayrton Senna.

Patrese, meanwhile, prepared to pick up some cards and enter the poker game. Threatened drivers drive so fast that they prove to the team they can't be let go. During the Hungarian Grand Prix, team orders might demand that Patrese throw his cards away and let Mansell win, but would he? Just to mingle uncertainty with uncertainty, the special fuels that all suppliers made were now banned. Experts estimated that this might cost the Elf runners (Mansell, Patrese) up to a second and a half a lap because Elf fuel had been so potent. Initially that seemed to be happening. In the Friday morning free practice Berger moved consistently into the 1:17s while Mansell needed 13 laps to get there and Patrese 22. Patrese, however, peaked at 1:15.882, the only driver below 1:16. Mansell was fourth.

During this free practice, a further uncertainty revealed itself. The kerbing round the Hungaroring had been removed to accommodate the motor bike Grand Prix on 14 June — the balance of a racing bike doesn't appreciate kerbs — but Hungary in summer is arid, parched and dusty. The kerbs acted as a boundary line separating the dust from the circuit. Without them, an errant car running only a fraction wide brought dust back, and that's slippery. In this session, the dust sent Senna, Brundle and Hakkinen off.

The two Williams emerged from first qualifying as the front row of the grid, Patrese provisional pole (1:15.476, Mansell 1:15.643, Senna 1:16.467).

Mansell's insight: *'I had some exciting times in the traffic, but I have to say on 16-lap-old tyres I was very happy to do a 15.7. One of the troubles here is that there are no kerbs on some of the corners, so there are no apexes. People are putting wheels off and you can come across dust clouds on flying laps. I had a little misdemeanour, my fault totally. I was pushing on tyres that I thought had come in but they hadn't.'*

It always seems to rain at Spa and this time Mansell was second to Schumacher.

Reportedly on the Friday night there were 'very heated' discussions between Mansell, Frank Williams and Patrick Head about the contract for 1993 and how much Mansell was asking. Estimates put that at 23 or 26 million dollars, depending on which rumour you listened to.

Mansell suffered more problems in second qualifying. It proved to be 'a big lottery getting clear laps and there were many, many accidents. I had one at the end. I came round on a very quick lap, there was dust on the circuit and I lost the car.'

Patrese	1:15.725
Mansell	1:15.950
Senna	1:16.267
Schumacher	1:16.524
Berger	1:17.414

The received wisdom about the tight and unyielding Hungaroring was that, like Monaco, pole man ought to reach the first corner first and win the race from there, the rest jostling and grumbling along behind. Thierry Boutsen had achieved exactly this in 1990 when he was trying to salvage his career with Williams. The received wisdom is not infallible, however, but 50–50:

	Pole	*Winner*
1986	Senna	Piquet
1987	Mansell	Piquet
1988	Senna	Senna
1989	Patrese	Mansell
1990	Boutsen	Boutsen
1991	Senna	Senna

Behind this list lay a much more interesting fact: Piquet had been on the second row in 1987, Mansell the sixth row in 1989. Pole helped but in no sense guaranteed anything, and, anyway, Williams would issue no team orders. Brown says that 'we didn't really have any major problems with the car that weekend although you always have something to worry about. He wasn't on pole, which I worried about a bit, but he didn't have to win the race to win the Championship.'

Reportedly that Saturday night more 'very heated' discussions took place between Mansell, Williams and Head. Much later, Mansell said that 'looking back, I feel the relationship between me and the Canon

Williams Renault team started to break down at the Hungarian Grand Prix. A deal was agreed with Frank Williams before that race — in front of a witness — and I have to say that at that time I felt very good about racing again with Williams in 1993.' Subsequently, too, Williams said that 'I was always optimistic throughout the summer until we got to the Hungarian Grand Prix, when financial considerations of a negative nature had to be taken into account. We didn't think we could afford everything being asked of us.' The contract moved into abeyance.

On the Sunday Patrese announced his intentions — 'I'm going for the win.' On the grid Jonathan Palmer of the BBC sneaked a brief word with Mansell, asking him how he felt. 'The most important thing is to wish my daughter happy birthday for today. She'll be over there in the Isle of Man glued to the television no doubt, so many, many happy returns of the day and we'll be with you later. We're going the conservative route [with tyres] because we are starting at the front, but we'll see what happens during the race.' Mansell sounded comfortable. The modulation of his voice was as we had so often known it, flat, factual, monotone, everyday.

Reflecting much later, I wondered if Palmer felt he was taking a chance approaching Mansell at such a charged moment. Since Palmer's reply broadened into such interesting areas, I reproduce it in full. 'I don't think I was taking a chance. Nigel has always been very good with the media. He recognises that the media have an important role to play. I must say that in my days as a pit-lane interviewer I found Nigel most co-operative, and had I not done so I would have hesitated about going up to him on the grid prior to the World Championship-clinching race. In general he had a lot of inner confidence and he certainly had there.

'Habitually he was very calm before a race — in so much as he managed to keep space for the media and his family and other things. He was very good at compartmentalising it when he got on to the grid. After that off he went into the race and he was obviously into his own world and his own working environment. There's something else about the Hungaroring you must remember. The Championship looked very strongly his and there were many more races left in the season in which he could have clinched it. We're not talking about a 1994-type Adelaide shoot-out between Hill and Schumacher.

'Having been on the grid myself as a driver, one knows what it's like and hopefully my time doing pit-lane interviews enabled me to empathise with the person I was interviewing. You can read the body language. The guy who's in the car, helmet on, gloves on, looking with a glazed expression straight ahead is not the guy that you really want to interrupt unless you've a producer banging away saying "We must have him! We must have him!" People do react to this pressure point [a few minutes before the off] by expressing themselves as themselves. In that area Nigel has always been very good — the compartmentalising, and having a compartment for the media.

'In my recollection, he didn't get tense on the grid. If anything he was pretty relaxed. He took the whole thing very much in his stride because he was a mature man and he did have, and I'm sure still has, this inner confidence in what he can do. There he did not feel that he couldn't allow himself a friendly chat with a mechanic or an interview — and he's always been eager to convey himself and his feelings to the public through the media. That day in Hungary, as far as Nigel was concerned, he'd done the qualifying bit, he was happy with his car in the morning warm-up and there weren't any problems. One of

The hairpin at Spa.

Inset *Data gathering, Portugal.*

Main picture *Putting the data to good use, Portugal – by winning.*

the great things about being on the grid is that chances are, unless you do have a problem, all the decisions which need to be made will have been made.

'Nothing preoccupies a driver more than the pressure to contribute to a decision-making process. That is at its peak after the qualifying sessions and maybe the morning warm-up. Once the driver, with his engineers, has decoded what he's going to do — run these tyres, that downforce, those ratios and so on — it is important for the driver not to have second thoughts immediately before the race. That is just a dreadful way to go in: being insecure, not having confidence in the car. You begin worrying about something and you can't do anything about it. You need mentally to put it to bed. Right, that's it, that's the car, that's done. Hungary was an example. He'd made his bed, it was good, so he was content to wander round and freshen his mind with other matters, not dwell on the car, which might give rise to self-doubt. It's often helpful to have something else to occupy your mind so you don't ask yourself "I wonder if . . ."'

On the grid, as he prepared for the summit, Nigel Mansell did not know that Ayrton Senna had had a very illuminating chat with Palmer's BBC comrade James Hunt. Nobody knew, except Ayrton Senna and James Hunt — and, a few moments after that, Murray Walker. Senna had not shown his hand but instead passed the hand to Hunt to show for him. We shall see.

'Yes, I knew James was going to make an announcement on air during the race,' Walker, sharing the commentary with Hunt, says. 'My personal view is that Senna knowing James, and knowing the effect it would have, deliberately told James knowing James would blow it all over the place. I am convinced Senna sought him out. And of course when James had got something like that, he couldn't contain himself. Probably I was the first person he told, but he was very full of it before the broadcast.' When the cards hit the deck they'd detonate.

At the green light Patrese placed the car cleanly into Turn One in the lead, Senna and Berger conjuring carving, tightening arcs round Mansell. Exiting Turn One after this convulsion of movement, Mansell had been rammed back to fourth: no consolation that only Mansell had ever won a Grand Prix at the Hungaroring from a position like that; no consolation because the Williams held superiority over every other car in the race bar one, that of his team-mate, the nice but now extremely determined Riccardo Patrese. Brown reflects that 'Nigel was completely boxed out of it at the start and we thought "This is going to be a bit difficult", but he'd a long way to go and he was in one of the two quickest car out there so he should be OK.'

As leader, Patrese enjoyed clear track — he forged a hunk of a gap instantly, this lap one — while Senna and Berger kept Mansell in jail behind them. The McLarens were slower, and up there Patrese demonstrated how much slower, but Mansell had to overtake them, which is not the same thing. In his candour, Senna confessed that 'I did not expect to win and I knew, to have a chance, I would have to get into the lead at the start. I made up one place going into the first corner and tried to stay with Riccardo for a single lap. I realised there was no way and I concentrated on running the race within my own limitations.' Patrese, just this once in a race of his own, travelled quicker and quicker.

Mansell accelerated up to Berger, Schumacher circled hungry behind Mansell, but these were only positions within a permanent panorama. Actually it was a prelude, but nobody knew that. You fell back a bit, you drew up a bit, you fell back a bit again: the Hungaroring can be like an accordion and just as predictable. By lap seven Mansell drew full up to Berger and the permanence of the

People power, Japan.

prelude was over. Moving into Turn One to start lap eight, Mansell — muscular, as they say — inserted himself and his car inside Berger, who did not resist. Mansell set off after Senna and drew full up soon enough. Senna accepted that, but, like Monaco, insisted the racing line belonged to him and kept Mansell in jail. At eight laps Patrese led Senna by 12.549 seconds and Mansell by 12.871.

Each moment that Senna held Mansell, Patrese became more remote, more uncatchable. To reinforce it, Patrese set a new fastest lap on nine, increased it again on 11. Repeatedly Mansell lunged into Turn One, repeatedly Senna said "No". By 12 laps Patrese, placing the car so surely that he seemed a man merely confirming his worth rather than issuing proclamations about it, increased his lead to 18 seconds over Senna, 19 over Mansell.

Mansell did not know, and neither did anybody other than Patrese, that Patrese's engine 'started to go after 20 laps and I had the feeling then that I couldn't finish the race.' The deceleration was almost imperceptible but the timings reveal it. On lap 20 Patrese did 1:21.994, new fastest lap. Then

Lap 21   1:22.172
Lap 22   1:23.311
Lap 23   1:24.382

The engine came on strong next lap — 1:21.053 — fastest of the race again. Patrese moved into great uncertainty and pressed forward, waiting to go to jail himself despite a lead over Senna of 21.249 seconds. While Patrese moved into this uncertainty, Hunt, talking live on BBC television, played Senna's hand. Hunt revealed the chat and revealed that Senna had revealed he would drive for Williams free in 1993 or, as Senna explained it, 'I will drive for the Williams team for 23 million dollars less than Nigel Mansell, or whatever Mansell wants. I am prepared to drive for Williams for nothing.' (Some said the sum was £12 million, but never mind). Senna, via Hunt, did not mention Prost. Hunt ruminated on the options and vented criticism of Mansell demanding so much money — or rather speculated on the Williams team's feelings on Mansell demanding so much money.

Right *Pulling power, Australia.*

Walker feels that Senna selected Hunt because 'of course it goes straight to the ears of the teams that Senna wanted to be most involved. It was a typically astute, self-centred and ruthless move, too. He wouldn't have driven for free. He would have got all his other money [sponsorships, etc] and he would have got that £12 million somehow from somewhere else. Nevertheless it was a brilliant political move. I didn't know when James would drop it into the commentary because you can't pre-plan those things, but I knew he would drop it in.' There had to be rich irony here, too: Hunt, the last Briton to win the Championship in 1976, creating mayhem for the man who could become his successor by afternoon's end.

The Championship looked inevitable — then he got a puncture

Patrese, pressing forward, increased the lead over Senna to 26 seconds. On lap 30 Mansell made a mistake out at the back of the circuit and ran wide, enough to allow Berger — tracking, waiting, tracking — clean through. Mansell was rammed back to fourth. The position after 32 laps:

Patrese	44:25.968
Senna	44:30.948
Berger	44:32.504
Mansell	44:33.082

On lap 34 Mansell retook Berger — muscular, again — on the inside at Turn One, although Berger squeezed him for an instant, moving across: Mansell third. Enjoying a clear track until he caught Senna, Mansell pressed out fastest laps on 35 and 38. A lap later the Championship broke open. Patrese spun on the downhill run out of Turn One approaching the next left-hander. 'I think there was some dirt on the track. There was nothing I could do.' Patrese rejoined, but seventh and with a push from marshals that might have disqualified him anyway.

Senna stretched from Mansell, Senna searching out the win in the snake of a track among the hillocks. 'I wasn't sure if second place was good enough to win Nigel the title so I asked on the radio and they told me yes. I knew that even if he came close he wouldn't take any chances. I decided to go for it and try to open a gap because I was worried I would have no tyres by the end.' Mansell need simply follow Senna at a prudent pace and a prudent distance and the Championship would inevitably follow. From laps 39 to 61 Mansell did that — and the Championship broke open again. Mansell had a puncture and, surely, had memories of Adelaide and the blow-out in '86, everything coming monstrously round again.

Brown remembers that 'Nigel came on the radio saying "I think I've got a puncture", and so we stared over the pit wall and there was the tyre all sort of grey in the middle and black at the shoulders. Yes, he'd a puncture.' Lee Gaug of Goodyear explained that although there was a cockpit warning light they taped it over because 'it can scare the hell out of a driver and it can be a false alarm. However, they knew about Mansell's problems in the Williams pit.' They did, and not just because they'd seen it. Patrick Head crackled on to the radio ordering Mansell in and ordered it so trenchantly that one wag suggested Head didn't need the radio. 'I was going round slowly and in I went. They could tell from the telemetry.' Williams also gave Mansell a pit board instructing him to come in because, as Brown says, 'We always do that. It's insurance if the radio has packed up, it's to be doubly sure.' Mansell remained stationary for 8.71 seconds and emerged to this race order: Senna, Berger, Schumacher, Brundle, Hakkinen, Mansell. He dug in hard.

Lap 63   1:18.308
Lap 64   1:18.852

On that lap Schumacher slewed on to the grass at Turn One when the rear wing failed and the G-force plucked it clean from the car, flung it away. That lifted Mansell to fifth. He advanced on Hakkinen at 3, 4 seconds a lap. Crossing the line to begin lap 66 — Patrese finally retired — Mansell needed third for the Championship. He dealt with Hakkinen to be fourth. He took Brundle at Turn One next lap to be third. He tracked Berger for a couple of laps and pitched the Williams inside at Turn One. 'When Nigel came up behind me he was going really quickly and I realised I had to give away second place.'

Brown says that 'Nigel needed to be third, but for some reason Patrick thought he had to be a place ahead of that to win the

Championship and told him over the radio. We had a system whereby we kept track of who was where in the race. I'm too busy looking after the technical aspect, trying to run the car, so Peter Windsor [the team manager] took care of that. The agreement was that we'd give Nigel an OK sign on the bottom of the pit board provided he was in a position to win the Championship. We'd been showing him OK for a long time but after the puncture he went out and he was not in that position of being OK. Then he started overtaking but Patrick told him over the radio that he needed to overtake Berger. And he did. And it was a good one! In fact Nigel finished with more than the required margin and he handled the final stages really sensibly, not trying to catch Senna. There's no point in risking flying off and breaking your wrist. If you do that you look a bit of a chump . . .'

Mansell looked anything but that as he smoothed and soothed the car safely home. That was the happy hour, the vindication, the consummation and the summit. He followed Senna to the end, a meaningless 40.139 seconds behind. In the proper historical context, which we can see now, he drove the race like a Champion and handled its reversals like a Champion. On a circuit where the received wisdom is that you can barely overtake, he had overtaken

Former motor bike champion Barry Sheene, who commentates on Australian television, finding out.

Berger three times, not to mention Hakkinen and Brundle once each. Not every Champion has won their Championship like this.

The immediate aftermath surrendered to emotion as it was always going to do, Union Jacks waving everywhere in the communion in a place so far from Silverstone, Mansell standing on the podium like an exhausted Hapsburg Emperor waving his finger to make the figure '1'. 'Afterwards was great,' Brown says. 'We all leapt up and down and went YEEHAA. I met him coming back from the Press Conference. I was wandering up and down and somebody said "The drivers are coming". I slapped him on the back and said "Well done". He was chuffed to bits, absolutely chuffed to bits. Very, very emotional, oh yes. No tears, but very, very happy.'

Mansell attended to the niceties and flew back to the Isle of Man for his daughter's belated birthday.

The leaving of the Hungaroring is no different from any other race. Everybody wants to get out at racing speed and from a euphoric multitude to emptiness takes about 20 minutes. Then you taste silence and see only stragglers. However, *Motoring News* reported: 'Senna is believed to have had a meeting with Frank Williams immediately after the Grand Prix but their discussions — inside a car in the paddock — were interrupted by an Italian journalist. They are then said to have concluded discussions over the telephone later that night. Mansell, also seeking an audience with Williams on Sunday night, was apparently rebuffed.'

Frank Williams would say that 'when somebody like Senna says "for free" it gets everyone's attention, including this company's attention.' Williams would add that the priority — that August evening — remained to have Mansell and Prost for 1993 although he did concede Senna's offer was 'an element'. It is something Ayrton Senna must have known it would be: a goddamned big element — like Pavarotti singing for a season no charge, Boris Becker playing a season for charity, Arnold Schwarzenegger destroying tower blocks with his bare hands for philanthropic reasons.

The team left the Hungaroring to catch a plane that night. The excitement was not over yet. 'We flew from Budapest,' Brown says, 'having taken the rather dangerous escorted police convoy through the middle of the city. The police go crazy and you have to try and keep up with them.' Murray Walker 'flew home that night, which is unusual for me, and stayed at London airport.'

Next morning, while Brown awoke with a hangover — 'quite a considerable one. Why not? A championship doesn't happen very often' — Walker took a plane straight to the Isle of Man. 'I interviewed Nigel at his home at Port Erin. The BBC had pre-prepared a Nigel Mansell World Champion programme which was going out on the Monday night and they stitched the interview into it and it made a wonderful ending. He was in his very best form, oh yes. Brilliant. He wasn't flaunting anything, oh no, he was what I would regard as his normal cheerful bullish self.'

A storm broke over Williams, an outpouring of rampant nationalism

---

A small group of journalists travelled there, too, and Mansell said, 'I am better and more courageous racer than he [Prost] will be if he is in Formula 1 for a lifetime or another ten years. He will be more of a chauffeur, making sure the car does the work for him. I can carry a car round but it is more tiring. When we were together at Ferrari I was very uncomfortable. I could not compete technically on any level. This time he is in an English team [Mansell had accepted Prost was coming] and I have had six years with them [Williams]. Alain has more to lose — I don't think he appreciates how much better a driver I am now. If anything goes on, all the engineers will come running to tell me in a second. On paper Alain is the greatest driver in Formula 1 with 44 wins, but his reputation has not done him proud. Getting fired from the most historic team, Ferrari [in 1991], is not exactly the best way to leave motor racing. I don't know how he has done it, but to get back and pick the best team and the best drive is some achievement.' Mansell added, 'It is Williams or nothing. If I am afforded the opportunity to drive with the same chances and freedom as this year then there is no problem. If not, then even more today than two years ago I would think about retiring.' He expected the deal to be completed within the week.

Reflecting, Frank Williams has said (in a BBC interview), 'We didn't think we could afford everything that was being asked of us. After Hungary it stalled, which was sad because there was poor communication between us until the Italian Grand Prix [on 13 September]. I think by then Nigel had made up his mind he wouldn't stay with the team and also would quit Formula 1. I became entrenched and obviously he did the same. He's a very obstinate, strong-minded individual and our minds didn't meet.'

Mansell later claimed that 'three days after Hungary I was telephoned by a Williams director who said he had been instructed to tell me that, because Senna would drive for nothing, I, the new World Champion, had to accept a massive reduction in the remuneration from the figure agreed in Hungary. If I did not Senna was ready to sign "that night". I rejected this offer and said that, if these were the terms, Williams had better go and sign Senna.'

By the Belgian Grand Prix, the race after Hungary, Senna accepted — *force majeur* — that Prost had an exclusion clause that prevented him from joining Williams; he, Senna, spoke of having a year off. In Belgium, Mansell finished second to Schumacher, but said, 'You will agree that there is incredible confusion, and Riccardo and I are probably the last to know what is going on.' Leading up to the Italian Grand Prix, rumours circulated that Mansell was talking to the Newman-Haas IndyCar team, which Michael Andretti was leaving to join Marlboro McLaren. Paradoxically Mansell would be joining Michael's father Mario, whom he'd partnered when he entered Formula 1 in 1980.

On race morning at Monza, Mansell announced his retirement and gave a long, embittered vindication and explanation. By now the remnants of the poker game bordered on farce. While Mansell made his statement a Williams employee advanced upon him and — live on television for all the world to see — placed the final Williams offer before him. Mansell rejected it and continued to read his statement. The Williams team reacted swiftly with this statement:

'Williams Grand Prix Engineering Limited deeply regrets the announcement today of Nigel Mansell to retire. Nigel has won 26 races for Williams, and our association together has been extremely fruitful. Everyone at Williams thanks him for the remarkable efforts he has put in and we wish him a happy future in his retirement from Formula 1.'

A storm broke over Williams, an outpouring of rampant nationalism based squarely around this: how can a British team not retain a Brit who's just won the World Championship? Moreover Mansell

The enduring images of the season: a gorge of water, a wave, a win.

issued a long statement. In it he said:

'Any relationship between a driver and an F1 team is vital for success and partly dependent on money — because it defines how seriously the team and its backers take the driver — but those who know me well understand the importance of the human side and the mutual trust and goodwill and integrity and fair play that are the basis of all human relationships. All these issues have suffered in recent weeks.'

It also said: 'To say that I have been badly treated, I think, is a gross understatement. Of course a team owner — any team owner — is free to chose whomever he likes to work for him. It was the lack of information, and the sudden changes, that I have found disappointing.

'It is difficult to put into words the sort of commitment you have to make in order to succeed in Formula 1. I am aware of criticisms made of my approach to racing. But I am the way I am because I believe in total sacrifice, a total ability to withstand pain and a total belief in myself and my ability.' He added, 'In the most sincere of ways I will be always grateful to the Williams team and to Renault for the support they have given me.'

Williams had to respond, particularly with the storm sending waves over the factory wall — one newspaper organised a demonstration outside. On September 15 Williams countered:

'Williams Grand Prix Engineering would like to re-emphasise its deep regret in Nigel Mansell's decision to retire from Formula 1 at Sunday's Italian Grand Prix. His 26 wins while driving for Williams allow him a special place in our history, having won considerably more races than any other of the team's drivers.

'To ensure the team has the best chance of winning races and World Championships, fellow director Patrick Head and I have always sought to employ the best drivers and engineers. To allow us to express our skills as engineers we have had to raise significant funds to invest in World Championship winning technology and World Championship winning drivers. This only comes from many long hours of considered negotiations which are dependent on many variables, some known, some unknown. Our strategy for 1993 included ensuring that we had Nigel in the team, a strategy we

Right *A rare study of 1992, Patrese in front. This is Brazil.*

pursued right up until Nigel's announcement on Sunday. Without going into details of the long and protracted meetings, we have made several offers to Nigel, all of which were rejected. Some criteria for the decision-making progress have changed throughout the year, but we repeat Nigel was the focus of our efforts for the 1993 season.

'In parallel with the driver negotiations, we obviously have to ensure the team's future, which in a world recession is difficult even with our World Championship winning status. It is noteworthy that despite the enormous support for both the team and Nigel from many British fans, we are still unable to raise any significant sponsorship from the UK. Our first responsibility is to Williams Grand Prix Engineering and its 200 employees and, therefore, regrettably we could not meet Nigel's demands in the time-frame required. We are obviously aware of the disappointment that Nigel's retirement generated in the UK, but Williams Grand Prix Engineering is an international company that operates on a global basis and must continue to do so.

'In the meantime, we would like to thank Nigel for all his efforts for the team and the sponsors and wish him and his family well in America. Nigel returned to the Williams team for the sole purpose of winning the World Championship and he has now achieved this goal. In doing so he has won a further 13 races with us, and this year has equalled the record number of eight wins in the season with three races still to go. We know that in the early months of his second period with us he said he would retire if he won the Championship. This could have obviously been a stronger consideration than we originally thought and whatever the final reasons for Nigel's retirement we are glad he has won the Championship he richly deserved.'

Williams did not sign Senna but did sign Prost. Mansell held the right cards at the wrong time, and whether he tried to put them on the table is irrelevant. They'd taken the table away. In the autumn of 1992 Mansell signed a seven million dollar one-year contract with Newman-Haas. As his Formula 1 career ebbed to an end this particular time round, he won Portugal, led Japan until the engine failed and was involved in a crash with Senna in Australia. Angered by that, he said he was glad to be going. Deep down I always knew he would have to go like that: spurned, aggrieved, unbowed, drawn into his own strengths: bloody-minded. He'd need that over there, all right; but, as the playwright said, he had it.

• CHAPTER THREE •

The Championship Over There

THE ANNOUNCEMENT THAT Nigel Mansell intended to contest IndyCars unleashed a bizarre palpitation amongst Britain's popular newspapers, who scarcely knew what IndyCar racing was. These papers discovered it was dangerous. The *Daily Express*, for instance, carried four stories on Saturday 19 September 1992, and I reproduce the headlines, the sub-headings and the first paragraphs of each.

YOU FOOL NIGEL
Warwick rocked by Mansell Indy move
Nigel Mansell's decision to join the daredevil world of IndyCar racing was last night condemned by his former Formula One colleague Derek Warwick.

I'D HAVE HIM BACK
Nigel Mansell's team boss Frank Williams last night reacted with disappointment to his defection to the Indy circuit.

MAIN ATTRACTION
Mansell can be a big hit with lovers of danger
Nigel Mansell's fast, aggressive driving style should have the money men beating a path to his door.

HE'LL BE CHEATING DEATH BY LESS THAN A SECOND

You can be a milli-second away from paying the ultimate price on IndyCar racing's biggest day.

The main concern centred around the oval tracks that IndyCars used for some of their races, and which were completely unlike anything Mansell had confronted before. Speeds exceeded 220 miles an hour and the ovals demanded their own distinctive techniques with fine margins of error. They were flanked by solid walls and Eddie Cheever, once of Formula 1 but now an experienced IndyCar practitioner, said memorably, 'Run-off areas are strictly a state of mind'. Of the 16 races in the 1993 season, from 21 March to 3 October — and with the month-long Indianapolis 500 as the centrepiece — six would be ovals, five street circuits and five road.

The cars were different and of this Cheever struggled to find a proper comparison. 'Comparing apples and oranges is wrong. Picking between oranges and nectarines would be more accurate.' IndyCars had turbos and ground effects, were heavier and not as nimble as their Formula 1 cousins. Cheever estimated the weight at 40 per cent more than a Formula 1 car. 'If you had a big accident at Indianapolis with an F1 car, there would be nothing left at all. You would just pick up the pieces with a broom.'

Mansell was not, of course, a pioneer. Among others with long (or brief) Formula 1 careers he'd meet Raul Boesel, Emerson Fittipaldi, Bobby Rahal, Teo Fabi, Danny Sullivan, Cheever, Stefan Johansson and Olivier Grouillard — as well as Mario Andretti, his team-mate, of course. He'd also meet home-grown talent such as Al Unser Jnr and Paul Tracy. Cynics suggested that IndyCars represented a retirement home for Grand Prix drivers. Frank Williams was quoted as calling it 'parochial. It is not technically challenging. I think when Nigel starts racing he will demonstrate that the level of driving is not the same as here. He may struggle on the ovals but his success on road and street will be enough.'

Mansell had joined a leading team. Paul Newman, co-owner, actor and occasional competition driver, described Mansell's arrival as

Right *He'd come a long way from the Lotus days.*

'incredibly exciting'. Newman adored racing and when he was once asked if he had any regrets he replied yes, he wished he were Mario Andretti, but 'I guess I don't wish it hard enough or fiercely enough. I enjoy the people in racing, for the most part, more than the people in Hollywood. There's a lot of "bull" in racing, but it's fun, put-on "bull".' (That's another difference. Newman couldn't have been discussing Formula 1.)

The Newman-Haas team was born in 1983 and won regularly. Carl A. Haas, the other co-owner, is nicely captured by the team itself. They have described him thus: 'Known for his trademark unlit cigar, Haas's low profile — at least in contrast to Newman — is intentional. His approach to the sport is simple and direct. "Racing," Haas says, "is a business." Haas directs that business from a state-of-the-art 32,000-square foot facility in the northern Chicago suburb of Lincolnshire, Illinois. While Haas travels extensively, he is far from distracted by the color and pageantry of the sport. "I've been around long enough that the racing scene doesn't excite me," Haas admits. "The fun, the only real fun, in racing is winning. Racing is a business, totally, and finishing second is nothing. You still lost. If you win, Sunday night is fun and it might even carry over to Monday morning. Then, it's work again."'

Mansell would have to learn new tactical thinking, itself an IndyCar art form. Races could and would be run under full course yellow flags if cars crashed, which meant following a pace car in race order until the debris had been cleared away. That invited pit stops (because you'd lose less time while the others circled so slowly), but when to risk those pit stops and what were the others going to do?

IndyCar itself adored the immediate legitimacy and publicity Mansell's presence brought, and so did the Newman-Haas team who reported on January 11, almost breathlessly:

'Phoenix. The 1993 PPG IndyCar World Series is more than two months away from its first green flag and yet a record has been set by Kmart/Havoline Lola drivers Mario Andretti and Nigel Mansell. Some 80 members of the working news media — about half representing organisations outside the United States — were at Phoenix International Raceway last Thursday and Friday (January 7–8) as Andretti was scheduled to evaluate the

He'd come to be Mansell the Immense. This is the demonstration outside the Willliams factory at his controversial leaving.

new Lola and Mansell take his initial laps on an oval track. It certainly was the most extensively reported test session in the 81-year history of IndyCar racing.

'Rain and high wind limited Andretti to just two days of work with the 1993 model Kmart/Texaco Lola Ford-Cosworth earlier in the week. The 1978 World Champion and four time IndyCar titlist turned a 21.2-second lap on the one mile oval in less than 100 laps. Mansell, the 1992 Formula 1 world champion, officially began his IndyCar career on the 1.1-mile Firebird International Raceway road course in nearby Chandler, Arizona, on Monday January 4. Driving a 1992 model Kmart/Havoline Lola, he did about 125 laps over two days, getting a feel for the turbocharged Ford engine, manual transmission, and a car that weighs about 500 pounds more than the Williams Grand Prix machine he used to win a record nine races, 14 poles and the title last season.

'Weather conditions finally permitted Mansell to take to the oval late Thursday afternoon. Again using the 1992 Lola, he got down to a 21.4-second lap after less than 75 circuits, just one-half second off Michael Andretti's pole time here last season. Unofficially, that would have placed him fifth on the grid for last year's race.'

Mansell's insight: *'I think the biggest difference is hanging on in a straight line because the car is set up to turn into the corner. I'm having trouble finding the words to describe it. Mario took me round the circuit and showed me the pitfalls before I went out. That gave me confidence. I'd hate to come to an oval unprepared.'*

Jim McGee, the wise team manager — he'd been in IndyCar racing since the 1960s — says, 'The first time I met Nigel was the initial test we did at Phoenix. He came with Greg Norman. From then on, it was really easy: he was a really easy guy to get to know and to work with. I found him one of the easiest I've known.'

In February, Mansell tested at the Phoenix International Raceway, using the 1993 car. On the Tuesday he set an unofficial track record of 20.6 seconds, a speed of 174.75 miles an hour. The official record, by Michael Andretti in 1992, stood at 20.952. Mansell covered some 160 laps and expressed satisfaction. On the Wednesday the team

The driving forces behind the team over there: Carl Haas with obligatory cigar and Paul Newman.

Main picture *Pondering at Laguna Seca.*
Inset *Discussing at Laguna Seca.*

concentrated on race set-ups and Mansell covered around 290 laps, of which 200 were a simulated race.

McGee said, 'We wanted to give Nigel a good idea of what a race would be like. He did three parade and pace laps and a 60-lap green flag segment [green for go] before a 14-second pit stop. We simulated some yellows, about 15 laps worth, so Nigel could do some re-starts. I told him after the "race": Nigel, you won by four laps!' On the Thursday Mansell drove 90 laps, getting near the 20.6 seconds again and describing the test as 'fruitful'. He was feeling at home. 'I had a lot of confidence in the Newman-Haas team to begin with and that's increasing all the time.'

'Drivers are friendly to one another — it's a kind of travelling circus

Sullivan, once of Tyrrell (1983) put Mansell's performance into context. 'It's very quick but I have to explain a little bit to you about Phoenix. It's a fickle track, to say the least. It all depends on the day you're there and the time of day you're there, so the only comparison is what the other guys there at the same time are doing. I'm going to take you through this process and you'll understand why. When Mario and Bobby Rahal and a few other guys were there previously, the fastest anybody could go was like a 21.6 or a 21.7. That's with new tyres, end of the day when it's cool. They did nothing to the cars, they showed up next day and did 21.2. It's a funny track and I was trying to think if there was any track like that in Europe. It's so fickle we don't really go to any other place like it. Literally you can have a small cloud come over and the track can change by a couple of tenths, but Nigel did the time and it is a quick time . . .'

Sullivan put something else into context. 'Nigel seems pretty happy to be coming out here. One of the things is compared to Formula 1 — all the politics, all the stress, all the back-stabbing and everything which goes along with that — you don't really have. Drivers are friendly to one another. That doesn't mean that if you start banging guys around the friendliness remains, but it's kind of a travelling circus. Everybody's pretty much working together.'

Mansell also tested at Laguna Seca, California, breaking the lap record there (2.21 miles in 1 minute 10.9 seconds, against Michael Andretti's 1992 pole time, 1:11.185).

There remained, of course, the tactical pit stops. McGee reflects that 'Nigel didn't want to make the decisions because he was new and he didn't understand a lot about them. We would sit down in our meetings and plan our race strategy. His comments were always, "I'm just going to drive the race. You tell me what you want me to do and I'll do it." He never questioned any of the strategies. He did exactly what we wanted him to do and it worked out really well. He had enough on his plate because of the fact that it was all new — the conditions and the races; the track would change and so forth. He didn't want to get caught up in trying to plan the strategy.

'Also it would have been very difficult for him to follow what the other drivers in the race were doing in terms of strategy, but we could do that and we had a lot of experience. From the strategic standpoint, we never had a problem and it ran very, very smoothly. A lot of things enter into it and Nigel is such a smart person himself that he knew this was something which would take time and he didn't have that kind of time. He had the confidence that the people in charge would make the right moves.' And they did.

Round 1. Australian FAI Indy Car Grand Prix, Surfers Paradise, Queensland, March 21. Length 2.7 miles (4.4 km). Race distance 65 laps (181.6 miles/292.3 km).

On a street circuit with 90-degree corners Mansell stirred everything nicely by taking pole (1:38.555 against Fittipaldi, Penske, 1:38.882). Mansell mania transferred itself straight from Silverstone: the crowd up to 80,000, TV to 90 countries, banners insisting MANSELL — KING OF THE POMS.

He made an understandable mistake in the rolling start, braking to avoid the pace car, and that allowed Fittipaldi to nip into the lead. 'I learned a lesson, but I'd not done a rolling start since my karting days 22 years ago.' Mansell fell back to fourth, worked his way up, led from laps 16 to 18. 'I came alongside Emerson very conservatively, with a lot of tyre smoke. Down the pit straight, my tyres were going "ca-chunk, ca-chunk" and Jim McGee was yelling "pit, pit" on the radio.' Mansell overtook under yellow flags and Fittipaldi radioed his team to make a protest. Mansell explained that 'I'd been hanging on just to stop for the corner. I couldn't see anything.'

From the stop-go penalty, during which he was given fresh tyres and fuel, Mansell resumed fourth and cut through into the lead again by lap 22, which he held until lap 29 when he pitted for a suspected puncture. 'Coming out of the first chicane I had a big wobble, probably because I hit the wall.' Mansell emerged fourth again, cut through again and urged a 32-second lead to protect himself when he made his final pit stop. He emerged from that still 17 seconds ahead of Fittipaldi. It was enough, even though at the end he nearly ran out of fuel. He'd became the first driver to win his maiden IndyCar race since Graham Hill at Indianapolis in 1966, and he spoke of IndyCars as 'a breath of fresh air'.

Round 2. Valvoline 200, Phoenix, Arizona, April 4.
Length 1-mile oval (1.6 km).
Race distance 200 laps (200.0 miles/321.8 km).

In Friday qualifying Mansell went quickest, and again on the Saturday morning. He'd already broken the track record, but, with 10 minutes of the Saturday session remaining, he lost control in Turn One and struck the wall so hard he smashed a hole in it. 'The back end went away. I was on the throttle at the time.' He'd remember thinking he couldn't avoid the crash, remember ducking and then nothing until he regained consciousness in the helicopter taking him to hospital. He'd hurt his shoulder, suffered concussion and wouldn't be allowed anywhere near the race.

Boesel gave this context: 'We all know that Mansell is a very brave and quick driver. He tested a lot at Phoenix and he was extra-confident, but the problem with oval circuits is that it is very difficult to judge the limit. That's the most critical point. He also drives, I'd say, on the edge of oversteer and, I repeat, it's very difficult to judge when you need to re-adjust the car, or the point where you can catch it, if something goes wrong. He was on that edge. You always think that if you've caught the car once, twice, you can go further, but that's when the oval catches you. He went one step further because of his confidence and the car got away from him. OK, on an oval you run on the edge, but you need to find the limit then adjust the car so you can

Sharing a smile with one of the most famous smiles in the world.

catch it. I can't say how long it might take him to learn this because, after all, he's driven the way he drives all his life, but maybe this crash will make him learn quickly.'

McGee gives this context: 'At the time I said, "That's probably the best thing that could have happened", and I told that to him. "Nigel, from what I'm saying you may think this is not the best means of saying it, but that crash is the best thing that happened." On ovals, he didn't really know where he stood. On a road course you can get away with things, and you can do things, with a car. If you make a mistake you may drop a wheel off the road or even spin, but when you make a mistake on an oval you've got to pay for it. He was getting away with a lot of things in the car at the time that you can get away with every now and then, but sooner or later you're going to put yourself in a circumstance where things aren't going to be exactly the way you think they are. You may just be a little bit over the edge and when you do lose it you can't get it back. There's no way. There isn't a man alive who can react to that. After he'd crashed, he said, "I didn't even know I'd crashed, it happened so quick. I couldn't have done anything because I didn't know I was in trouble."

115

'Had he crashed at Indianapolis or a faster place than Phoenix it could have been more devastating because when you lose a car entering a corner that's when you usually kill the driver or that's when they get seriously hurt. They are carrying their maximum speed. He was entering the corner off the straightaway, hadn't scrubbed speed off, did half a spin and went into the wall backwards. Nigel knew about it after that and never came close to losing the car again on an oval. At Phoenix he went way over the limit. He was throwing the car in the corners and catching it and then finally he got so wide with his pattern, he got so aggressive with the car, that the car just didn't have the grip. It's understandable, oh absolutely.

'He felt there was a separation among drivers and we talked about that. He felt there were a few drivers in the world that could drive Formula 1 cars differently than any of the others, and that was himself, Senna and Schumacher. He felt they were in a class by themselves. He had figured out something in the cars that he could get away with more and drive the car harder. He was applying that to the ovals. After Phoenix he had a lot more respect for the ovals and I think he was a little reserved, which was in his favour. Still, it never affected his ability to go fast.'

Round 3. Toyota Grand Prix of Long Beach, California, 18 April. Length 1.5 miles (2.5 km). Race distance 105 laps (166.9 miles/268.6 km).

After Phoenix, Mansell spent two weeks in and out of hospital for treatment. 'I thought at Phoenix I was able to race the next day, but when I got home I went downhill for four or five days. It was the worst feeling I have ever had from racing. I'm still feeling the effects of the hit.' Mansell had been to Long Beach before, with Lotus in 1981, 1982 and 1983. 'I can't make any comparison. It's been such a long time and everything has changed so much because of all the construction in the area. It's as if I'm going there for the first time.'

Chris Pook, the race organiser, disagreed. 'He's going to recognise instantaneously eight very critical turns. He ran through the Hyatt Hotel's garage [where the track went] in 1983. That's been eliminated, but everything else is the same. He may say, "Gosh it's new". Sure, it's been ten years but every professional racing driver has the power of rapid recollection. By the third lap of practice he'll be there. The only real difference is that he'll be driving an IndyCar.'

In Friday qualifying Mansell had padding in the cockpit to soften the pain and the team used ice packs on his back after qualifying. Pook was right and Mansell took pole, beating the track record. 'When the race starts you ignore the pain. You just do your job and when it's over you can start worrying about the pain again on Monday.' He thrice led the race but finished third to Tracy (Penske) and Bobby Rahal (Rahal-Hogan). During it, however, Mansell and Unser (Galles Lola) had a coming-together that enraged Little Al. 'I set up Nigel high on the exit of Turn One and was ready to pass him on the exit of Turn Two. I've never seen anybody block me as bad as Nigel blocked me today. He knew exactly where I was when I was behind him. Then, as soon as I got beside him, he had no idea where I was. He parked me against the wall. Well, what goes around comes around.'

Mansell's insight: *'I didn't see what happened. I felt it but I didn't see him. He knew my reputation. I'm not going to move over. Al's a great*

IndyCar could barely believe the attention Mansell brought in his wake.

driver and I'm sorry he ended up in the wall. I don't think anyone can complete a passing manoeuvre there.' Mansell 36 points, Andretti 32, Fabi 26, Rahal 24, Tracy and Boesel 22.

Between Long Beach and Indianapolis, Mansell underwent back surgery in Clearwater, Florida. Before it he said, 'I have been in considerable discomfort since Phoenix. I am relieved that my latest set of X-rays have identified the exact problem and it is going to be corrected permanently.'

Round 4. Indianapolis 500, Indianapolis, Indiana, 30 May.
Length 2.5-mile oval (4.0 km).
Race distance 200 laps (500 miles/804.6 km).

Officials running Indianapolis granted a request by the team that Mansell be allowed to take three phases of the mandatory rookie [newcomer] test when he arrived at the Speedway rather than with the other rookies. What did that mean, apart from the obvious? Dick Jordan, communications director of the United States Auto Club, which makes the rules for Indianapolis, explained it. 'The rookie test is in four phases, but only the first three are completed before the circuit officially opens for practice and qualifying on May 8. The last phase, ten laps, is carried out after May 8. All we've done is let Mansell bypass the organised rookie session before then. From the rule point of view it's no big deal.'

The rookie test involves drivers covering speed-limited segments to prove that they can handle the car competently: ten laps in the 185–190 mph range, then 190–195, then 195–200, then 200-plus. Mansell duly passed. Qualifying, over four days and two weekends (May 15/16, May 22/23), is baffling until you understand it. The grid is decided on a descending order of *days*, so that a slow time on Day One takes priority over a quicker time on Day Two and so on. This explains why Day One is called Pole Day and why many drivers go all out for a time on Day One and then go all out to get home and relax, ignoring Days Two, Three and Four. On Pole Day, Mansell qualified eighth.

'I'm a bit disappointed but pleased and relieved that we're in. I'm a bit frustrated, a bit disappointed for the team, because we thought the car would be perfect for this time of day. We didn't change the car from lunchtime. When you do a 222.9 mph in the heat of the day, you tend to expect things to be the same. Instead we lost 3 miles an hour. We agonised for three or four hours about changing it. I was itching to go, like I have in all my career, because I'm used to having an hour instead of the whole day, but I was advised you could be quicker in the afternoon. Unfortunately the track changes. I was running out of road everywhere.'

Mansell headed for Clearwater and returned for three days of practice where he peaked at 225.468 mph. Discussing the race, he said that he intended to keep his eyes and ears open for the first 400 miles, then go for it.

Race day is a vivid panorama of marching bands, an Invocation by an Archbishop, 'Taps' (the equivalent of the Last Post) to commemorate America's war dead, a fly-past, and the singing of 'Back home again in Indiana'. The engines are started at 10.51, the parade lap 1 minute later, the lap behind the pace car at 10.58 and the race at 11.00 sharp.

Boesel took the lead, Mansell running ninth after being baulked in the rush. He worked his way up to lead on lap 70 — only the second

So much to learn, including the art of the tactical pit stop — Andretti shows how.

reigning Formula 1 champion to do that (Jim Clark the other, 1966). Mansell held on until lap 91 when, under a yellow, he pitted and overshot, emerging seventh. He'd lead twice more, 129–130 and 175–184, but be back to third behind Fittipaldi and Dutchman Arie Luyendyk (Ganassi) for the final rush. And this is what happened next . . .

Autosport reported that 'in Turn Two on lap 193 Mansell got too wide, running up out of the groove into what's called "the grey". Near the end of the corner he smacked the wall — a good one with both right-side wheels. Any incident of this type will result in an instant yellow at Indianapolis and the flags were waving from the starter's stand even as Mansell wrestled his car off the wall and kept going. With only seven laps to go, Mansell, determined to stay out, hit the brakes at the start/finish line to see if his car reacted in an untoward way. It didn't so he decided to carry on to the finish. The green flag waved a final time at the end of lap 195 and the cagey Fittipaldi had it

Phoenix, preparing en famille.

all sussed out. In Turn Three he slowed right down, dropping to second gear and forcing Luyendyk and Mansell to get out of the throttle at a crucial moment. "Emerson outfoxed me on the restart," Luyendyk said. "He did a fantastic job of coming to a complete standstill. I had to go to second gear and then I got sideways putting the power on. He got a couple of car lengths on me and that was the end of it.'"

One American wrote: 'After Nigel Mansell's debut at the Indianapolis 500 Sunday, all he could say was "I goofed". Well, he said a few other things, too, but not until he jokingly chastised himself for providing more than a few strange moments at the Indianapolis Motor Speedway. There was the time, for instance, when Mansell rolled past his pit in the middle of the race. "A rookie mistake," said Mansell, shaking his head between a couple of chuckles. "Hey, I just drove by. What a splendid fellow.'"

Mansell's insight into lap 195 and the Old Fox Emmo? *'I really thought I had gotten on the gas fast on the restart, but then, all of a sudden, I heard Voooomm. They were on the gas for three seconds before I even reached it. Big mistake.'*

McGee's insight into lap 195: 'Nigel could have won the race had it not been his first restart on an oval. He didn't know what to expect. Emmo took advantage, but anybody would — because Nigel was not aware of an oval restart. He'd never done one because he got hurt at Phoenix. He never had the opportunity to know how they group up and run. After that it was no problem.' Mansell 50 points, Andretti 43, Fittipaldi and Luyendyk 37, Boesel 34, Fabi 30.

Round 5. Miller Genuine Draft 200, West Allis, Milwaukee, Wisconsin, 6 June. Length 1.0-mile oval (1.6 km). Race distance 200 laps (200 miles/321.8 km).

Mansell took the lead with 18 laps left, going outside Boesel who couldn't re-catch him. I can't resist quoting Gary D'Amato of the *Milwaukee Journal*: 'OK, Nigel Mansell has gotten this oval thing down pat. Took a couple of weeks but, hey, nobody's perfect. So what's next? A little NASCAR Winston Cup action, perhaps? Mansell laughed at the suggestion, then rubbed his forefinger and thumb together. Mansell is British, but the sign was universal. Money talks. "Anything's possible," he said with a twinkle in his eye. Indeed, with Mansell behind the wheel of a race car — any race car — anything but everything's possible. "The feeling I've got is comparable, if not better, than winning a Formula 1 race," Mansell said. "I'm just very happy to have won today for the team.'"

'Next weekend after Indianapolis,' McGee says, 'we went to Milwaukee and it was the same circumstance again. Nigel was leading the race with about ten laps to go and it went yellow and then it went green. Man he took off! Boesel almost jumped him on the restart but Nigel knew what was coming so he made a great restart, which is just what he should have done at Indianapolis if he'd known.' Haas pointed out that 'when we came here, Nigel had never seen this place before. I was hoping to just get some points, but he goes ahead and wins the race.' Paul Newman added, 'Ditto. Mansell is more and more impressive every time he races.' Mansell 70 points, Boesel 52, Fittipaldi 51, Andretti 43, Luyendyk 37, Rahal 36.

Round 6. ITT Automotive Detroit Grand Prix, Belle Isle Park, Michigan, 13 June. Length 2.1 miles (3.3 km).
Race distance 77 laps (161.7 miles/260.2 km).

A road circuit, and Derek Daly, the former Williams driver and now

This is Phoenix, the oval circuit in panorama.

IndyCar commentator, said, 'Nigel has realised that oval racing is the best form of racing, the most enjoyable form — it's exactly how you imagined racing would be when you dreamed about it as a kid. Road racing is just violent physical abuse . . .'

A bit of that at Detroit. Mansell had pole but the Old Fox outjumped him at the start and, to forestall any mutterings, insisted, 'I did a good start and Nigel backed off. I've never heard of a race that didn't start with a green flag.' Tracy got by, too, Mansell shaking his fist at him. Later Mansell ran second being hounded by Johansson who complained that 'he was all over the place. His car was obviously a lot slower than mine. Sometimes blocking is just part of the game and I don't mind that, but he would miss a shift and then cut right over in front of me. It was ridiculous.' On lap 68 Mansell went off line and crashed. He left the circuit without offering any insight into anything. Mansell 71 points, Boesel 68, Andretti 57, Fittipaldi 51, Rahal 46, Luyendyk 37.

Round 7. Budweiser/G.I. Joe's 200, Portland, Oregon, 27 June.
Length 1.9 miles (3.1 km).
Race distance 102 laps (198.9 miles/320.0 km).

Mansell, pole again, led to lap 27 but the Old Fox kept nipping his tail — 'There were no tricks between us,' Fittipaldi said, to which Mansell added that they'd been 'just inches apart', but it was all fair. A mistake on lap 28 cost Mansell the race. He had a brake balance problem and under braking for the chicane slewed off, was given a stop-go penalty (any driver going straight on at the chicane received this) and rejoined fourth; charged, of course, got up to second by the end but too far away to mount a direct challenge to Fittipaldi. Mansell 88 points, Boesel 74, Fittipaldi 72, Andretti 65, Rahal 58, Unser Jnr 45.

Round 8. Budweiser Grand Prix of Cleveland, Ohio, 11 July.
Length 2.3 miles (3.8 km).
Race distance 85 laps (201.3 miles/324.0 km).

Early in the day (American time) the British Grand Prix was run at Silverstone, Damon Hill and Prost forming the front row of the grid in the Williamses. Graham Hill never did win this race, but Damon, handling himself with confidence, might now. The notion of a Brit holding a real chance of winning Silverstone had traditionally done magical things to the attendance, but you could see how much the absence of Mansell was being felt. The lager army stayed at home and rather than the roads being blocked, you could drive straight in and out of the circuit, an unknown luxury for a decade.

Later in the day (American time) and on the circuit of Burke Lakefront Airport, complete with sections of runways, the Penskes of Tracy and Fittipaldi were superior, as Mansell himself acknowledged. Tracy had taken pole from Mansell, Mansell took the lead and held it for 14 laps, Tracy from lap 15 to 30 (his pit stop) and from 32–60 (his second stop) and from 62 to the end: as IndyCar races go, surprisingly straightforward. It suggested a tightening on Mansell. If the Penskes held an advantage, they had the drivers to exploit that. Tracy, a pleasant bespectacled young Canadian, was ferociously fast but prone to error. If he was maturing out of that he had eight races to create something, not to mention the Old Fox, second, who professed that his car had been quicker than Mansell's and he had thoroughly enjoyed himself. Mansell 102 points, Fittipaldi 88, Boesel 80, Andretti 75, Tracy 62, Rahal 58.

Round 9. Molson Indy Toronto, Ontario, 18 July.
Length 1.7 miles (2.8 km).
Race distance 103 laps (183.3 miles/295.0 km).

In practice and qualifying Mansell crashed a couple of times while the Penskes strengthened and strengthened. Mansell ran to lap 55 but a wastegate problem halted him, Tracy winning from Fittipaldi. That changed everything. Fittipaldi 105 points, Mansell 102, Boesel 86, Tracy 83, Andretti 80, Rahal 70. Mansell pointed out that this was the first time his car had failed and he wasn't complaining.

Round 10. Marlboro 500, Brooklyn, Michigan, 1 August.
Length 2.0-mile oval (3.2 km).
Race distance 250 laps (500 miles/804.6 km).

Mansell responded to the Penske strengthening with a bloody-

Different backdrops.

minded blitz. On this bumpy oval, the Newman-Haas Lola was stunningly good: Mario Andretti pole from Mansell, Tracy fifth, Fittipaldi 15th. That was the story of the race, too, Andretti leading from Mansell and both pulling away from Luyendyk. On lap 28 Mansell went high into Turn Two and took Andretti on the outside. Immediately he forced a gap and the central issue became, astonishingly, whether Andretti could unlap himself — he'd gone a lap down on 102.

Andretti managed that on 145 and they ran to the end a lap up on Luyendyk, Tracy long gone (engine) and Fittipaldi grappling to find the right set-up. He finished 13th, a place from the points. Mansell sat for a time in the cockpit savouring the victory, then said it had been the hardest race of his career, harder even than any Brazilian Grand Prix in 120-degree heat. He also confessed that Michigan was 'the fastest circuit I've ever run', and the only way he could imagine preparing for 500 miles was to drive more and more of them.

'I'd judge it was his most difficult race of the season,' McGee says. 'He hadn't felt well, he had the 'flu and he threw up in the middle of the race. We kinda had to talk him through that whole race, but he won it convincingly by a lap and he was incredible there. That was his toughest race from an endurance standpoint and the fact that he

125

Left *Sometimes the strain showed.*

was so ill. After it he just fell out of the car and it wasn't an act, no. We gave him some aspirins in a water bottle during his pit stop because he had such a pounding headache. That place has a tendency to beat you down into the ground, anyway. People don't realise how ill he was. Half way through he was going to come in. He said, "I don't think I can make it." We said, "Well, just try and go a few more laps, just kinda feel your way along" — and he led the race almost all through. He was fast.' Mansell 123 points, Fittipaldi 105, Boesel 98, Andretti 97, Tracy 83, Rahal 74.

Round 11. New England 200, Loudon, New Hampshire, 8 August. Length 1.058-mile oval (1.7 km). Race distance 200 laps (211.6 miles/340.5 km).

Mansell prepared to celebrate his 40th birthday on race day and launched the initial celebrations by taking pole from Boesel (169.247 mph against 169.207), Fittipaldi, suffering boost problems, 13th. Mansell had taken some ribbing about growing old and, in his best humour, responded. 'I'll tell you a little story about my age. For five years when I was starting in motor racing I stayed 25 in all the newspapers and magazines, but someday you have to pay the bill. It was quite a jump when I went from 32 to 37 almost overnight. I've had a wonderful time and, I tell you, I've got to give credit where credit is due. It's not me, its the series, it's IndyCar, it's the officials, it's the public, it's even you gentlemen and ladies of the media; but above all you've got the people driving for the teams — these guys are some of the most professional, competitive guys in the world, period.'

The race lay between Mansell, Tracy and the Old Fox. Mansell moved into an early lead, Tracy took it up from laps 41 to 68, Mansell from 69 to 74, Tracy from 95 to 196. Tracy, combative, lusted past Fittipaldi for second place and sliced inside Mansell for the lead on that 95. A yellow flag on 145 meant that all the cars could complete the race without further pit stops and it became a shoot-out. The green flag released them on 156, Tracy swift to the power, Fittipaldi and Mansell comparatively slower. Mansell applied pressure to Fittipaldi and tried the inside at Turn One on lap 170. Fittipaldi blocked that robustly but lost momentum, which allowed Mansell through at Turn Three. 'That was one of the hairiest moments of the race. I went into the turn expecting Emerson to give way and he didn't.'

Tracy, up ahead, judged that Mansell's car was quicker, but he could hold him by being more creative in traffic. Mansell, however, drew up to him and on lap 190 seemed to have nosed ahead, but as they lapped Scott Brayton (Lola Ford) — Mansell tucking in behind Brayton — Tracy seized the outside. Blast, Mansell thought (or words to that effect), now I'll have to do it again. 'This is all about learning where to be half a lap ahead, like a chess game. I got past Paul and then forgot there was another corner coming up and he just blew right around me.' Mansell closed up and on lap 197 darted outside as he and Tracy prepared to lap Johansson — after making sure Tracy would go to the inside. 'When I saw Paul go down to the bottom of the track, I did it and it worked.' Tracy counter-attacked but Mansell resisted. Mansell 144 points, Fittipaldi 119, Tracy 100, Boesel 98, Andretti 97, Rahal 80. An American sportswriter, sharpening one of those sentences they do so well, and mindful of the 40th birthday, wrote: 'Nigel Mansell went over the hill at top speed Sunday . . .'

McGee judges New Hampshire 'the best race Nigel drove during the season. That's where he and Tracy had that duel with about ten laps remaining. Most people who saw the race thought it was the best oval race they had ever seen. With ten laps to go it looked like Nigel was all done. He was sitting back in third place and he was 4 or 5 seconds off Tracy and then, all of a sudden and out of nowhere, he caught him in traffic and passed him on the outside and went on to win. There was so much duelling and passing and traffic and everything that it was a fantastic race — and on his birthday, also!'

Round 12. *Texaco/Havoline 200, Elkhart Lake, Wisconsin, 22 August.*
Length 4 miles (6.4 km).
Race distance 50 laps (200 miles/321.8 km).

Tracy pole from Mansell, Tracy straight into the lead, Tracy not to be caught. Mansell went for points, which he got with second place but 28 seconds adrift, Fittipaldi fifth. The maturity of Mansell was evident. He didn't need to try and win everything everywhere, he could let the Championship fall to him rather than whip up a storm and risk the whole thing. He was 40, after all, and he'd been driving for a while: since his dad bought him a go-kart with a lawnmower engine before he was ten. Mansell 160 points, Fittipaldi 129, Tracy 122, Boesel 110, Andretti 97, Rahal 94.

Round 13. Molson Indy Vancouver, British Columbia, 29 August.
Length 1.6 miles (2.6 km).
Race distance 102 laps (168 miles/270.5 km).

Mansell struggled for grip, Fittipaldi couldn't get on the pace and they finished sixth and seventh. Mansell quantified the race as two points gained over Fittipaldi, Fittipaldi quantified the race as 'disappointing' and said that his tactics must now be to win the last three. Mansell 168 points, Fittipaldi 135, Tracy 122, Boesel 114, Rahal 111, Andretti 107.

Round 14. Pioneer Electrics 200, Lexington, Ohio, 12 September.
Length 2.2 miles (3.6 km).
Race distance 89 laps (199.3 miles/320.7 km).

It could have been settled here, although that seemed unlikely. To take the Championship Mansell must finish in front of Tracy and at least six places in front of Fittipaldi. Mansell took pole from Tracy and Fittipaldi, but it wasn't going to be that easy or that comfortable. The race started on the back straight, longest and quickest of the circuit, and fed the cars into esses. Here Mansell and Tracy collided heavily. Mansell claimed that Tracy 'chopped me right across the front of my car', called it 'unprofessional' and expressed the hope that Tracy hadn't done it deliberately. In many ways, and despite their age difference, they were similar in self-expression in a racing car, constantly searching out chances to be taken.

Mansell limped towards the pits and, during the journey there, Luyendyk clipped his car, damaging it further. Mansell lost a couple of laps in the pits while Fittipaldi pursued Tracy for the lead, but Tracy, trying to lap a slower car, went off. He departed the circuit without comment. Fittipaldi ran to the end to win, Mansell making a long, dogged slog to 12th and a point. 'I drove my heart out for that.'

Mansell astonished IndyCar by how fast he mastered it, particularly the ovals.

Afterwards, Fittipaldi insisted that Tracy hadn't been deliberate at the start — 'There's no way Paul would. I know that Roger Penske tells him never to get involved in anything like that. Paul was just trying to take the lead.' Mansell 170 points, Fittipaldi 156, Boesel 126, Tracy 122, Rahal 119, Andretti 113. Meanwhile, Donington announced that Mansell would be taking part in a Touring Car event on 31 October, driving a Ford Mondeo. In this unlikely setting, and so far away from Lexington, Ohio, the communion would be re-established.

Round 15. Bosch Spark Plug Grand Prix, Nazareth, Pennsylvania, 19 September. Length 1-mile oval (1.6 km).
Race distance 200 laps (200 miles/321.8 km).

It could be settled here, again. Mansell took pole from Fittipaldi and Boesel, Tracy fourth, but Fittipaldi made the better start, Tracy struck past and on lap four Boesel struck past, too. For Mansell the opening 20 or 30 laps were 'a nightmare of understeer. I had to rethink and redrive the car, altering my lines a little bit.' When he'd found that, he struck past Fittipaldi on lap 45 and Tracy two laps later to lead. He never lost it. He was in that mood. 'You never get a minute's peace. It was the greatest race and the most thrilling one I've ever been in from the point of view of pure racing, traffic and overtaking.' Only Scott Goodyear finished on the same lap. In Formula 1, Prost (ironically, of course, Mansell's replacement at Williams Renault) had all but won the Championship. After the Italian Grand Prix on 12 September: Prost 81 points, Hill 58, Senna 53. Prost could, and surely would, settle it at the Portuguese Grand Prix on 26 September. It meant that for one week Mansell held a Championship over there and a Championship over here.

'I've had five great feelings in my life, the births of my three children — and I was there for each of them — winning the Formula 1 World Championship and now winning the IndyCar Championship. When my wife and I came over here we wanted to enjoy ourselves. I wanted to be competitive and I thought we'd win a few, but I had a bit of luck along the way.'

McGee says that 'Nigel was so dominant at Nazareth that it probably wasn't as good a race as he ran in New Hampshire. We had some

Real speed, Toronto (Allsport).

problems with the car that weekend. In fact we had an engine problem and he didn't practice very much in the car that he raced — only ten laps or so — and then in the race the car ran flawlessly and he was so dominant he could lead any time he wanted and he did. It was one of those days when everything goes your way. He was ecstatic after he'd won and realised he'd won the Championship. He's probably the only one who will ever hold the two Championships simultaneously. That was great.

'I ran Emerson's programme when he came over here [in 1985] and Emerson is a great race driver, but it took him a long time before he felt comfortable with the IndyCars — like three years. Everybody thought Nigel would do well on the road courses, but when it came to the ovals he would have his problems. It was just the opposite. He dominated on the ovals but the car wasn't as good as the Penskes and so forth on the road courses. We were always playing catch-up. Nigel's the best, and I mean that of all the guys, he's just an incredible talent.' And the context of winning over here and over there back-to-back? 'It might be done by an IndyCar driver who goes to Formula 1 and wins that and then comes back and wins this as Mario [Andretti] did, but to win Formula 1 and win IndyCars next season — never having driven them before — is, I think, a feat that may never be repeated.'

The 1993 Championship duly won, Haas confirmed that Mansell would remain with the team for 1994. 'I'm very gratified to have Nigel back, very happy to continue the relationship. We had an agreement for 1994 but we both wanted to extend beyond that time. That meant a number of changes in the current contract. I never thought I would lose Nigel. Next year will be easier for him. He will not have to learn the race tracks. Every place we went was a totally new experience for him this year. If we give him decent equipment he should go quicker next year.'

Mansell's insight on staying: '*A lot of thought went into this. Carl and Paul got me over here. We wanted an extension for all the right reasons. The friendship and support of the Newman-Haas team and the sponsors were second to none. I've worked with some megabuck sponsors in Europe*

Right *The car readied before the Championship clincher, Nazareth* (Allsport).

134

and the ones we have here are the best I've ever been associated with. It's a family unit with Carl and Paul and myself and gives me an opportunity to compete at a higher level. I've been with Ferrari, Lotus and Williams, probably three of the greatest in Grand Prix history. My relationship with Newman-Haas is second to none throughout my whole career. Carl means almost as much to me as the late Colin Chapman, and Colin was virtually like a father.'

What was it like coming over?

'There was a personal adjustment that was ongoing. I was like a fish out of water. I learned more sayings. My naivete was very illuminating. Our barometer is the children. All of our comfort zone is getting better. I'd thought I might do one year of IndyCars, not like it and then retire for good. I like this series. Look at all of the Formula 1 drivers here this weekend. That's a tribute.'

In the final race, at Laguna Seca, California, on 3 October, Mansell and a backmarker, American Mark Smith, collided after 71 laps. Mansell was not pleased. But it didn't matter now. His position in history was safe for ever.

• CHAPTER FOUR •

Leaving and Returning

THE EVENTS OF Donington Park reflected Nigel Mansell in many of his aspects. The specific event, a Touring Car shoot-out, had a format tailored to television with a variety of regulations to ensure close racing. Dave Fern, the circuit's Press Officer, captured one aspect. 'Nigel handled the weekend perfectly from the moment he arrived. That was the Friday morning. He arrived at the circuit at 9.30 and immediately a little lad recognised him. The lad asked for his autograph and wanted it on a picture of Mansell. 'Sorry, but it's a big photograph,' the lad said. It was unrolled across the roof of Mansell's car and he signed, and he kept on signing autographs all weekend. He'd come to meet his fans.' Ah, the communion.

His presence drew a crowd of 63,000. Without being provocative, more paid to witness him in this relatively unimportant form of racing than had paid to watch the British Grand Prix. Moreover, the 63,000 represented double the number of spectators at the European Grand Prix at this same Donington the previous April. Here was another aspect. Mansell, created by Formula 1, had outgrown and overgrown it to a domestic audience.

In the shoot-out final Mansell suffered a misfire and fell back, charged to fifth, charged to fourth and, bringing the crowd to tumult, set fastest lap. Tiff Needell, driver and television person, captured the next aspect. Mansell 'dive-bombed' him for third place into Redgate but got sideways out of the Old Hairpin. In grappling to correct that, Mansell went across Needell's Vauxhall Cavalier, which rammed him. The ramming pitched Mansell across grass and into a wall. He struck it so heavily that he rebounded towards the track and had to be cut from the wreckage. A section of the crowd called obscenities at Needell, moved by the same mentality they'd shown at Silverstone in 1992 when they invaded the track, no doubt.

During the weekend, Mansell explained that although his immediate future lay in IndyCars, he did not preclude a return to Formula 1. He could spend a quiet Christmas and prepare for the first IndyCar race of the new season in March. While he did that, few guessed that the Newman-Haas Lola would be off the pace in 1994 or that Mansell's love affair with IndyCar would degenerate into what someone has described as a divorce. To compound this, the Penske team — with three strong drivers, Fittipaldi, Tracy and Al Unser Jnr — dominated, sometimes absolutely.

On 20 March Mansell finished ninth in Australia; on 10 April, third at Phoenix; on 17 April, second at Long Beach. He prepared for Indianapolis 500 practice to begin on 7 May. By then everything had changed. On 1 May Senna died in hospital after crashing in the San Marino Grand Prix. A whole dimension in Grand Prix racing died with him. Damon Hill, partnering Senna at Rothmans Williams, could not be expected to replace it in essentially his second full season; nor could young Schumacher at Benetton.

The natural, evolutionary cycle of the sport had been destroyed at Imola. Evolution more or less guarantees that the tiny number of great drivers will be superseded by others about to become great themselves: a constant regeneration and one that maintains overall interest. Between them, Prost, Senna and Mansell won every Championship from 1985 to 1993 (except Piquet, then at the end of his evolutionary cycle, in 1987). The Prost v Senna v Mansell struggles, feuds, strifes and turbulent triumphs kept the overall interest heightened; but Mansell had departed for IndyCars in 1993, Prost retired at the end of 1993 and now Senna had been taken in the third race of 1994. What did that leave? Schumacher led Hill 30

Right *Detroit 1994, the Penske cars rampant.*

points to 7 and threatened to make the remainder of the season a very long procession.

In due time Williams confirmed that test driver Coulthard would partner Hill at the Spanish Grand Prix on 29 May. By then the hard word was that Williams wanted Mansell back, and that Renault — disquieted that Schumacher would win everything with a Ford engine — wanted Mansell back. Certainly Bernie Ecclestone of the Constructors' Association, a man concerned about the overall interest, wanted Mansell back, and said so. Haas, understandably, pointed to Mansell's contract and the fact that the pivotal event of their calendar, the 500, was upon them.

What could be more gratifying than Formula 1 admitting that it needed *him?*

The hard word hardened that Mansell might contest the Grands Prix that did not coincide with IndyCar, France, the European in Spain, Japan and Australia. What could be more gratifying to Mansell than Williams, the team he felt had spurned him at the moment he ascended the summit in 1992, reaching out and embracing him again? What could be more gratifying than Formula 1 admitting that it *needed* him? And, because he would bring to Formula 1 what no other driver on earth could bring to it — and everyone knew that, not least the marketing men — he could demand (and get) a fortune. Some would speak of £1 million per race, others $1 million. (If you're on £25,000 a year, it takes 40 years to earn £1m.)

First, however, he must contest the Indy 500. At Indianapolis he spoke of the Imola tragedies. 'I'm sitting here talking to you this morning and I don't really want to believe it has happened. There is a tremendous void in Formula 1. The last week or so has been one of the saddest in my career. There's a very big element of luck involved and when the luck runs out then it's down to the engineering of the car, so if you have a very bad accident the engineering really comes into play. While luck is on your side you can have a mediocre car and get away with a lot, but when that luck runs out you pay a high price.'

On 26 May he made a formal announcement under the weight of so much speculation. 'Formula 1 has gone through tragic times in recent weeks. Against that background and bearing in mind our successes in the past, it was perhaps inevitable that speculation would take place about the possibility of people trying to persuade me to return to F1 — despite all the problems that would cause. After all, I have often said that in motor racing, anything can happen!

'On Sunday, however, there takes place the most important race in the world. I am contractually committed to Newman-Haas Racing — and personally committed to Carl Haas and Paul Newman, to my engineer, and all the guys who work so hard to make my car competitive and safe — to give all my effort for preparing for this race.

'So I hope it will be understood that I will spend no time thinking, still less talking, about Formula 1.

'Regarding this matter, I have nothing to add at this stage.

'Thank you.'

On May 27, two days before the race, Mansell appeared for a hook-up Press Conference between Canary Wharf, London, and Indianapolis. He was in his best laid-back form.

Having won championships on both sides of the Atlantic, if you win on Sunday, what's going to be the next big challenge for you?

'I think every race you go into is a very big challenge, I think your motivation is looking forward, not behind, although we have won two championships as you quite rightly said on both sides of the Atlantic. Every race you win is something that you add to the history books, but there is no question I would be one of the happiest people in the world if I could actually win on Sunday. All I can tell you is that I shall be putting all my efforts, endeavours, skills and thoughts into the race this coming weekend.'

Have you not thought of any further challenges beyond winning the Indy 500?

'Well, I know that's a good question but you can only focus on something that is within reach, within a few days or a week. If you are trying to focus competitively, you can only tangibly plan something which is close and prepare yourself for that. After this event is over, I will look to the future again — Milwaukee the week after. I would like to win there. I won there last year. The event after that is Detroit, and not until I've got what they call these treble hitters out of the way will I focus on what I want to do for the immediate future or the long-term future.'

You have said that Indy has had three different race winners so far this season, and F1's only had one. Have you any ideas how that can be changed?

'Which particular part, change what?'

Well, can we get somebody to beat Michael Schumacher?

'It is very difficult. You have to look at everything. It's rules and regulations. I'd answer it this way: when you stand still in motor racing you go backwards. I think it's for all the teams, whether it be this side or the other side of the Atlantic, to get together and agree a strategy and a basis of rules where people can compete closer and it's not dependent on how much budget you've got. You mustn't take it away from the Benetton team, they've done a fantastic job and they've deserved every bit of success that they've had this year, but it's a very good question. I think it requires everyone who has the knowledge and the answers to get together in a room and agree a sort of formula for the future where people can compete and it will be a lot closer.'

The family would be back soon, though not to Monte Carlo.

On an oval track, what's the difference mentally going round and round compared to a normal circuit?

'Well, here you are averaging over 220 mph all the time, you are going down the straights and slip-streaming at 240 mph-plus and you've got a 500-mile race or 200 laps to complete on Sunday. So you've to keep your concentration for three hours and you can't rest for a second. Even along the straights, the car's trying to turn left because the car is pre-loaded to go around the left-hand turns. You've got to have a completely clear mind, you've got to be totally focused, you haven't got to have any other thoughts than the Indy 500. Come Sunday, if you allow anybody or anything to disturb your mental preparation you're doing yourself an incredible injustice and, more seriously, you can put yourself in jeopardy of making a mistake.'

Is that any different to when you are on a Formula 1 circuit, or is it the same?

'The thing is, you're going into every turn — 1 and 2, 3 and 4 — at 200 mph-plus. When you're on a normal circuit you have a variety of corners. You might be 180 mph around one corner, then braking down to 160/140 mph for another, and you're going around bends. Here a little bit of complacency can come in if you are not concentrating or focusing and all of a sudden you can get bitten real hard.'

Aspects, aspects. In the race Mansell was black-flagged and given a stop-go penalty for passing Boesel after the pit lane blend line [explanation in a moment]. Later, under a full course yellow, the car of an American rookie, Dennis Vitolo, ran into — and onto — Mansell. When he'd been led away to safety Mansell exploded. 'Apparently he has just been on television and admitted responsibility. Apparently he said on television he was going miles too quick and he braked too late and the next thing he knew he was on top of me. What can I say? I was just following everyone else slowly around in the slip road to the pit entrance. The next thing I know, I was sort of going half-backwards with a car on top of me on fire. I've got a slight concussion. That much I know because I'm nauseated. I feel sick.

'I'm just so disappointed. We got back up to third place. Everything was looking good. We were going to get back on the same lead lap. There's no words to express the disappointment and the surprise. I've never had an accident when you've been under a yellow flag. It's just unreal. The thing was, the impact when he hit me — he probably hit me in excess of a hundred miles an hour more than I was doing.

'Suffice to say that I'm upset and I'm going home. I was getting burned a little bit. The fumes came into the car. I've just upset all the medical people. They want to take me to the hospital [meaning a regular hospital] but I just want to go home. I've got my doctor friend there and I'll go back to his practice when I get to Clearwater, just to have a look at things. I'm almost in shock being put out of the race under a yellow flag.'

Vitolo (who 'didn't know Mansell, I hadn't ever spoken to him') remains convinced that the accident, one of the most astonishing even of Mansell's career, was the product of 'a set of circumstances. A yellow flag came out from an accident in Turn One and we all slowed. Going down the back straight I was catching up the field, John Andretti in front of me. Soon after the yellow came out there was another accident in Turns Three and Four with John Paul Junior and as I came along the back straight they were putting all the cars down on to the warm-up lane [which runs round the infield from the pits and can be used in emergency to get cars away from debris on the track]. What I think happened — and this is just what I think, not fact — is that, when John Paul Junior crashed, the safety vehicle came out across the warm-up lane.

He was obviously upset, talking to himself — 'I can't believe I'm out of the race'

'The pace car must have stopped or gone very slowly to let the safety vehicle go across. All the race cars were bunching up like an accordion but we still weren't completely bunched, everyone was catching up. As I came around the inside of Turn Three — because we're closer to the fence now — John Andretti was going almost 20 miles an hour, almost dead stopped. I came around blind and as soon as I came around he was right there. I got on to the brakes — carbon fibre brakes, they were cold — and it just didn't stop. I couldn't slow in time and my right front hit his left rear and that launched my car up. It went past Scott Brayton and then the bottom of my car landed on Mansell's left rear tyre. Once it got on the tyre, that rotated my car on top of his engine cover. I couldn't believe it, because we were going so slow. I'd been talking to the pit crew along the back straight and they were saying, "Do you want to make a pit stop?" I slowed, I was waved to the warm-up lane and boom. It all happened within a matter of a second or so.

'I was talking to my pit crew on the radio telling them what had happened and letting them know I was OK. I said, "I still don't believe this, but I've just had an accident going slow." I think Mansell's car had a small turbo fire, which is common. Then Mansell jumped up and jumped out and one of the rescue people was running towards him and they ran into each other. They rolled on the ground a little bit. I stepped out of my car without a problem. After any incident at all at Indianapolis you have to go back to the track's hospital. I sat opposite him in the ambulance. It was an uncomfortable journey for me, yes, it certainly was. He didn't say a word to me. He was actually pretty quiet. He was obviously upset, as I was; he was talking to himself. "I can't believe I'm out of the race." That was it. He was pretty calm. He was fine when we went into the hospital together and it wasn't really until afterwards that all the commotion started. By that time we were pretty much separated and gone our own ways. To be honest, I can't remember saying sorry to him — not that I recall, anyway. I don't think I said anything.

'USAC has timing beams all the way round the race track and I thought maybe I was going too fast. I'd been racing at 200 miles an hour and now, going much slower, maybe I'd misjudged my speed, although I felt like I was going very, very slow. The timing beams gave my speed at 71 miles an hour coming into the warm-up lane. The speed limit in the pit lane is 100! They said, "You weren't going fast, you were going relatively slow", and I said, "That's what I thought." One thing I do remind people is that, no matter what happened and no matter what Nigel said, it wasn't his fault. He had a right to be angry, there's no doubt. The words he spoke? I mean, there's not much I could do about that. It's easy for someone who's a World Champion to bash someone who's unknown. What can you do? There's nothing you can do in that situation.'

Team manager Jim McGee puts the Indy 500 into context, and to do that he embraces 1993 as well as 1994. 'In 1993, going from the crash at Phoenix right to Indianapolis, the job he did was impressive.

Patrick Head makes points.

The first year he handled the whole Indy 500 scene very well, but he was hurt after Phoenix and he didn't spend a lot of time at Indianapolis. The next year, 1994, is when he had more of a problem. He was there and he had too much time on his hands. It's not his type of atmosphere, you know. He doesn't like to hang about, he likes to come in and get the job done and at Indy there is so much hanging around [over the month], it rains and the wind blows and you get yellow flags and this and that; but to be fair it would be the same for every Formula 1 driver, and that's what got Piquet hurt [in practice in 1992 when he crashed at 220 mph].

'I kept telling Nigel at the time. I said, "Nigel, all of this that happens, all the build-up. I understand, to me it's a pain, too, but you can't let it affect you." You focus on that [the periphery] and you lose your focus on what you're really doing here, and that's what happened to Piquet. He was so aggravated by yellow flags and track clean-ups and everything like that, that he wasn't focused on what he was doing and he ended up crashing and it crippled him. So my main consideration and job with Nigel was to keep him focused. All year that was part of my talk to him. "Forget about what's going on around us, let's stay concentrated on this deal and let's get out of this thing without anybody getting hurt." A lot of the real success at Indy is from the guys who are able to push all the rest of this stuff aside and not let it bother them. You let that stuff get to you and next thing you know you're not thinking about what you're really there for and there is a tendency for you to get lost or make a mistake. The first year wasn't bad because he was hurt from Phoenix; he came in and he did his qualifying, couple of days practice and he went home to help recoup, came back for the race and so he only spent like four or five days there — last year he spent almost twice that amount and it really just worked on him. But he still did a great job in the race. I mean, had he not had the problems and the guy who ended up on top of him, he could have won, oh yeah. We were the fastest car there and we had just got back on the lead lap after the stop-and-go penalty.

'It's funny because at Phoenix this year [1995] Art Meyers, who was the chief steward, came to me and apologised for the problem we had with the black flag. He said it never should have happened and only did happen because of the way the race track was laid out. They made a mistake in the fact that the pit lane blend line [separating the pit exit from the track] was too close to the first pit and it was impossible for any driver coming down the pit lane to judge whether he was in front or behind the guy leaving the first pit box because of the speed difference. You're coming down the pit lane 80 miles an hour and the guy leaving the first pit box is at 20 miles an hour. How do you know whether you cross the line with him or behind him or in front of him? You don't. They made a mistake. What they needed to do was move that line at least a couple of hundred feet. That kind of soured Nigel. He felt as though they were against him, which they weren't. He felt that maybe they were picking on him, which they weren't. The Speedway people thought Nigel was great and he was great for the Speedway.'

What effect would the return of Mansell have on Hill's title attempt?

At Milwaukee Mansell finished fifth and divorce proceedings began. He'd written a letter to USAC expressing his feelings about allowing a rookie like Vitolo into the Indy 500 and, overall, this may have been a mistake. Whatever the accident at Indianapolis had been, the American public — and particularly conservative Middle America — didn't expect it to be recycled on and on and didn't expect USAC to be implicitly criticised. Moreover, Mansell expressed (in quasi-diplomatic language) to the media that he was less than thrilled with a car that couldn't get near the Penskes; and David Brown of Williams attended Milwaukee. He and Mansell were seen in conversation. Frank Williams, canny as usual, refused to lend it significance . . .

Mansell drove the Rothmans Williams Renault in the French Grand Prix on 3 July. Coulthard could scarcely complain at being temporarily replaced, although, on his debut in Spain, he ran sixth early on (the electrics failed) and in Canada fourth in front of Hill, who fumed. Coulthard finished fifth.

'At the time I was very disappointed,' Coulthard says, 'because at the point where I was replaced by Nigel I was already doing a reasonable job for the team. My feeling was, "Well, why do you want to change it?" I was also aware that Nigel hadn't only signed for Magny-

Cours but the last three Grands Prix of the season.' (The extent of the Mansell deal was kept in a dark place.) 'So I knew straight away that I'd only be doing eight Grands Prix that year, and although it wasn't made public that he had signed for the last three races, I think people had heard of it.'

Of greater importance, what effect would the return of Mansell have on Hill and Hill's championship attempt? Hill has written (in his book *Grand Prix Year* with Maurice Hamilton, Macmillan) that the decision was a commercial one pressured by Renault. While he understood that, it still felt like 'a kick in the crotch.' Reflecting further, however, Hill realised that he could increase his stature by beating Mansell — not least because Mansell was earning more from this one race than Hill for the whole season.

Authentic Mansell Mania descended upon the broad, lush acres of Magny-Cours. In first qualifying Schumacher took provisional pole, Hill third, Mansell seventh; on the Saturday Hill took pole — just.

Hill	1:16.282
Mansell	1:16.359
Schumacher	1:16.707

The Old Boy could still put a hot lap together. You see, many judges wondered if IndyCars had blunted Mansell's fine edges, if the years after his 40th birthday were moving against him in a significant way, if the Return of The Immense would be as sad and humiliating as returns can be. Mansell's riposte lasted precisely the 1 minute 16.359 seconds. Successively, Mansell gave these insights. After first qualifying: '*I am very pleased because the result with the limited laps isn't too bad. I still haven't got the right balance on my car, but it has a big potential. I have to settle in now and see what I can do tomorrow. I feel optimistic I can do a lot better. It is a very big challenge. I stated that before I came here and I am not disappointed in any way.*'

After second qualifying: '*Following yesterday I'd have been happy thinking I could stay in the first six, so I am proud to be next to Damon. My first run was on old tyres and I had to abort because of traffic, then when Damon got pole that really motivated me. Damon did a great job and deserves pole.*'

Hill described his — Hill's — last run as 'beautiful, a bit desperate at times, but exciting . . .'

In the race Mansell ran third but the pump-drive went on lap 46. He thanked everyone and departed for America without further ado 'because I've got a race in Cleveland next week'.

After first qualifying there: 'I can say that Formula 1 cars are much more hectic but I don't want to come back to the United States and start comparing cars. The biggest difference is in braking. In Formula 1 you go much deeper into the corners, but to me a race car is a race car. I went to France to have a good time and I had a lovely time. My comfort zone in the car over there was 1 or 2. Here it is an 8 or 9.'

During the race Mansell and his team-mate Mario Andretti had a meeting of machinery, not minds. Mansell gave his testimony. 'My team-mate side-swiped me. I hope it wasn't on purpose. He should watch where he is going.' Andretti gave his testimony. 'Nothing broke on the car, well, nothing broke until I got hit. The car Number One [Mansell] miscued there a little bit and hit me on the left front and it broke the wishbone. I'm sure he didn't want to do it but he should have been more careful. I was just passing another car and I

A little advice for Damon Hill before the Adelaide shoot-out?

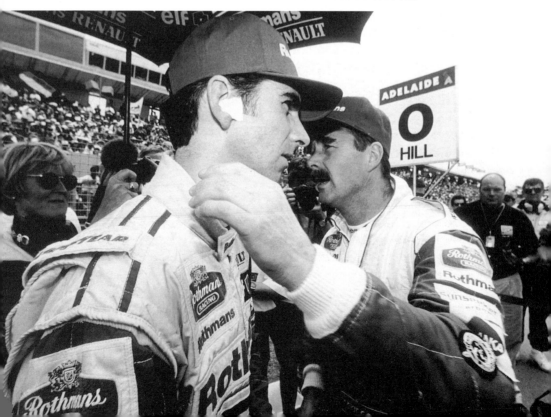

got a little extra bit off camber off the corner. He sort of took advantage on the exit to get by me. I got hit real hard.' Mansell finished second to Unser. 'I drove my ass off in the race. I feel very satisfied with the result.'

Eight rounds remained, and Mansell's season drifted. He took nothing from Toronto, nothing from Michigan, was seventh in Mid-Ohio, took nothing from New Hampshire. The divorce was officially announced soon after.

'Lincolnshire, Illinois. Newman-Haas Racing today [30 August] announced that Nigel Mansell will not return to the team for the 1995 PPG IndyCar World Series. Carl A. Haas said on behalf of Newman-Haas Racing that Mansell has expressed a strong desire to return to Formula 1 racing. Haas said the team does not wish to stand in Mansell's way and his release will become effective after the final race of the 1994 IndyCar season.

'Newman-Haas Racing and Mansell made history in 1993, when Nigel became the first reigning Formula 1 World Champion to switch full-time to the IndyCar circuit. He went on to capture the PPG Cup title — the first true rookie ever to do so — and secured five wins en route to Driver of the Year honours.

'"Paul Newman and I have enjoyed our success with Nigel," said Haas. "We became friends. Along with our major sponsors, we thank Nigel for his contributions to Newman-Haas Racing and the world-wide attention he brought to the PPG IndyCar World Series. We all wish him the best of luck and success in the future, and I know our friendship will continue."'

Mansell took nothing from Wisconsin and nothing from Nazareth, where he was asked if the Formula 1 press would be expecting derogatory statements about IndyCar. 'I've tried for two years to tell them over there how good the series is. Have you read anything derogatory from me? About my motivation — well, Emerson and I feel we could take anyone on. I won't have anything but praise for this series. I'll miss the jokes that we can exchange and the banter among the drivers. I expect it will be more serious over there. The drivers get on a bit more here.'

He came eighth at Laguna Seca, the final IndyCar race, which gave him a week to get to Jerez for the European Grand Prix. The adventure in the New World was over. Naturally Haas and Mansell made the right noises. Gordon Kirby, a highly experienced American reporter, however, reviewed the season for the British *Autocourse* annual and suggested that once Mansell thought he had a Formula 1 contract for 1995 he 'refused to test for Newman-Haas any more and also argued privately and publicly with team-mate Andretti'. Interestingly, Bernard Dudot, the Technical Director of Renault, says, 'I have always had great admiration for Nigel, especially for the pleasure he gets from his driving, but if the car is not going well he loses all of his motivation.'

At Jerez Mansell was sixth in first qualifying and moved to third next day. 'It was an exciting session. I can't remember being in one like that. It was like playing poker, when to go and when not to go, when you could get a clear lap.' In the race he spun off. 'The back end got away from me and I just lost it, simple as that. It was a big moment.'

The first real evidence that he might still be competitive in Formula 1 was delivered at a rain-sodden Japanese Grand Prix, stopped on lap 15 and restarted, aggregate times to count. Mansell spent most of both legs challenging Alesi's Ferrari for third place. This was good stuff, as James Hunt used to say, Mansell probing, Alesi clenching his teeth and holding his nerve and defending, late braking against later braking — but neither man making a single unfair or unwise move. The Old Boy could still put a combative race together and go to the end of it. On the final lap Mansell did get through and punched the air because he'd be on the podium, but 'I forgot that the race was on aggregate so he beat me in the end!'

In Australia, in first qualifying, Mansell took provisional pole and also spun avoiding the spinning Benetton of Johnny Herbert. 'You have to have a sense of humour when you come round the corner full bore and see the track blocked. That was a close moment and I was happy to be able to do a time after that. I gave myself a lap to settle down and then I tried to give it the big one and it was just quick enough.' Rain washed away the second session. Mansell kept pole, the 32nd of his career. Aye, still put a lap together . . .

Inevitably the world watched Schumacher and Hill go head-to-head for the World Championship while, at the start, Mansell had a skirmish with the scenery. After Schumacher and Hill crashed, Mansell went head-to-head with Berger for the vacated lead and they enjoyed themselves, Mansell pressuring Berger into a mistake and taking the win. The podium was a happy place, Berger ribbing Mansell about his age. At the post-race press conference, Schumacher, drawn between many emotions as the first German Champion, couldn't bring it into any sort of context and asked Mansell about that. 'It gets better,' Mansell replied, grinning broadly.

How did Coulthard view all this? He had, after all, been obliged to view it in the literal sense. When Mansell signed, 'I knew that I had eight races to try and prove I was good enough to be in Formula 1, but I was also aware of the fact that people have short memories and three races [Jerez, Japan, Australia] is a long time not racing, and Nigel doing good performances, which undoubtedly he'd do. Balanced against that was me losing the potential to race. I had to prove in my eight races that I was capable of racing for a top team in Formula 1 and show the potential because winning is so difficult, you know — it's not easy.

'There is something special about Nigel, the way he motivates people'

'I'd met Nigel many years ago when I was racing karts and he came to Silverstone to do a promotion for a gentleman I raced for, Martin Hines, who knew him. Way back then — I was about 14, 15 — of course I was in awe. He was already winning Grands Prix, he was the type of guy who always gave 110 per cent in the car and it was fantastic to meet someone and touch them and find they were only human. It was all the things you get the first time you meet somebody famous.

'I got on with him in 1994 absolutely, no problem whatsoever. I know there was this thing at the end of the season — sort of keep Coulthard out of the pits and all that sort of rumour — but I've never had one bad exchange of words with Nigel at all. He's never been anything but friendly with me so I still have the same respect for him.'

What did you notice about him driving your car?

'You watch even closer. There is something about Nigel which is very special, the way he motivates people round about him and the way he is able to bring the focus of all the people to him. It's some-

153

Inset *Victory, Adelaide.*

Main picture *Old boys' reunion. Mansell congratulates Berger on coming second.*

thing special that he has: whether that's born of experience or whether that's born out of his personality, you can't help but notice it. It was interesting to watch him working with the team off the circuit as well. The thing that gave me a lot of confidence was that he wasn't going any quicker relatively — relative to Damon — than I had been. That did give me a lot of confidence. After all, he has proved he can win races, proved he can win World Championships, and I haven't proved anything yet [pre-season 1995].'

Did you not see anything specific about the way he drove your car, like, for example, going into the corners deeper?

'If Nigel felt you really cared about him, he needed nothing else from you'

'I wasn't able to get that sort of information during the race weekends because everything is so intense and the last thing you want to do is tread on the feet of the engineers or the drivers — I appreciate that being a driver myself. I kept out of the way to let them do the job. It's so difficult to see anything on the track. You can see Alesi in-car and his hands are going like this, and you can see maybe a little bit of the car twitching — but it's not like the old days. Oversteer for us is different. In the old days it was visual as the guy came through the corner. Nowadays, oversteer is huuuup and that's it, it's over. Today's car doesn't go sideways, it goes only one way and that's forwards.'

Frank Williams explores the Mansell context. 'Love or hate Nigel, he's news, isn't he? Nigel, especially during the last two races — Japan, Australia — was a total pleasure to work with. Nothing was too much trouble on or off the track. He was totally apolitical in the team, and he was a ball of fun the whole time. Really, really. No exaggeration. It was partly because he knew he had to help Damon win, so he wasn't at odds with his team-mates, which is the norm. We were very straight with him. He was happy, he was relaxed, he was well-paid in a competitive car and he began to get the hang of that car. He felt good. When he's in a normal wartime environment his attitude will be different, which is what makes him good.'

Did you find the real Mansell?

'If Nigel trusted you and felt that you were working for him he was a good guy, no question. That's the trick. Nigel is more mellow than he was three or four years ago, he's quite a different person. He learned a lot in America, no doubt about it. He was OK in '94 with us, he's relaxed.'

Grown up a lot?

'Yes, that's right. If Nigel felt that you loved him as a person and you really cared about him — and I'm not being cynical at all — he needed nothing else from you. He never needed to be told how good he was. He liked applause and adulation, loves it, but he needed to be sure that he could trust you. He just has a big chip on his shoulder. He thinks people are going to try and shaft him, but if he believes that the people are with him he's magic. He's got an enormous amount of inner strength, great confidence in himself.'

Did you feel that you had to man-manage him, keep building him up?

'He didn't need it, Ayrton Senna didn't need it, I don't think Alain Prost needed it, although Alain was probably suspicious of people, around him (initially).'

Does Damon need it?

'Good question. He's very introverted, he doesn't talk much, but I don't think he needs it either.'

Aspects, aspects, always. Whatever, a chapter of the Mansell story — or saga — closed at Williams and another opened at McLaren. It would be, as we have seen, brief, and truly stretch your credibility.

• CHAPTER FIVE •

The Man in the Cockpit

THE EARLY LIFE and times of Nigel Mansell are well documented, perhaps exhaustively so: the struggle into motor racing, the crashes in junior formulae, he and his wife Rosanne selling their flat to finance a few races, the moment when Colin Chapman noticed him, the firing by Lotus, the ascent with Williams, which, in the space of six weeks at the end of 1985, altered everything and pitched him towards Immensity.

Those six weeks, however, remain largely unexplained. From the eternal loser, Mansell came second in the Belgian Grand Prix on 15 September, won his first Grand Prix in the European at Brands Hatch on 6 October, won again at Kyalami on 19 October and was on the front row in Australia on 3 November. He became one of the leading drivers in the world. Why and how? David Brown, you'll remember, began working with Mansell at Kyalami.

'He realised he could do it. All the time he'd kept saying I am capable of doing this and he was right. I think the same thing is true of a lot of drivers. They all drive because they believe they can win. Only a small percentage actually can. What is it? It's the *realisation*, it's the *proof*, it's an *awakening* that they're not getting pit boards saying P2 or P3 [you're second, you're third] any more. The driver awakens from that condition into "I've won the race". The confidence goes right up

The Mansell power, in wet or dry.

The man in the cockpit, and out of it.

and, particularly with Nigel, confidence is very, very important.'

I put the why and how to Keke Rosberg who partnered Mansell then. Rosberg had driven for Williams since 1982, when he'd won the Championship, and had mixed feelings about Mansell joining him for 1985. 'I'd say the performance of the team increased during the season. I had won Detroit [on 23 June], for example. The performance increase came half and half through Williams and Honda and we got some new pistons or something for Montreal [the race before Detroit]. From then on it was all much rosier. His emergence was the so-called confidence factor. You get on a high and your performance improves. This is what we saw with Schumacher last year [1994], it's what we were seeing in Damon Hill at the end of last year, beginning of this year and now with Coulthard.

'He'd created a lot of problems at Lotus — that's why I was negative about him joining'

'The problem with Nigel wasn't really his driving ability at the time, but he had created a lot of problems at Lotus and that's why I was a bit negative of him joining — well, not a bit, but very negative. Elio de Angelis [Mansell's partner at Lotus] was one of my closest friends in Formula 1 and Elio had warned me about him and said, "Look, the guy creates problems around him". I tried to prevent that entering Williams because we had a fantastic feeling in the team. I must say that Nigel turned any negative ideas about him to positive. We worked very well together, we drove our hearts out, but there was absolutely nothing negative.'

Why is confidence so important? 'Take Sergei Bubka in pole-vaulting. He does what he wants, can do anything. I believe that in every sport the mind is the thing that gives you that extra little bit. You can see Karl Wendlinger going downhill, you could see JJ Lehto going downhill last year — that's when the mind went the other way. The pressure grows, your performance is not completely what you expect and it snowballs and destroys you.

'My first and primary objective was to destroy Mansell like every other team-mate (chuckle). We worked very openly and honestly together but I never worked any other way. Maybe I was a bit too stupid not to use tactical and political advantage. I believe that's the way you get more out of the sport [being apolitical], but whether it's the most successful way I'm not quite sure.'

Alesi reminds me very much of Mansell. (It was before Canada 1995, which Alsei won.) If he could just win one race and calm down . . .

'. . . Oh yes, he'd be off. At the moment he's forcing the issue . . .'

. . . and Mansell did before he ever won. . .

'. . . Yes, but I did too. Then all of a sudden it starts clicking, the car, you, the team, everything. I felt a tension that Mansell had to prove himself in '85, very much so. Very much so. Once he had proved himself he didn't really relax, he just got hungrier and hungrier and hungrier all the time.'

I'd felt that tension in the early 1980s, Mansell on a lonely and sometimes derided journey, and arm-wrestling the odds along the way. If you were close to it, you found yourself associating with it, wanting him to emerge, wanting him to do it. Of the six-week emergence, however, Rosberg adds, 'Don't forget also what happened was that I was leaving the team and Honda played quite strong politics. We had enormous arguments about that. I would say that towards the end of the season Honda invested heavily in Mansell's future. They tried to make Mansell look as good as possible. But he took the chance, you've got to give him that. I give him all credit.'

Mansell was the first person in Formula 1 I ever interviewed, and I thought that if they're all like this I won't have any trouble. He was exceedingly polite and helpful. He spoke softly but firmly. He answered questions thoughtfully. He seemed relaxed in the way strong men can relax themselves although — it was Canada, 1982 — he had everything still to prove. I liked him and that wasn't difficult. He also had confidence: 'quietly confident', as the old saying goes. I won't bore you with details of how we fell out, because I've written about that before and once is enough, but it occurred in the late 1980s when Mansell could be testy, and sharp to any injustice perceived or real. Into the 1990s he could still erupt in extreme circumstances, but he seemed more easy in himself. He'd made the difference between starvation and staying hungry.

I was extremely curious to know what David Brown made of him, and for your interest this interview took place in April 1995. First, what is your job specification?

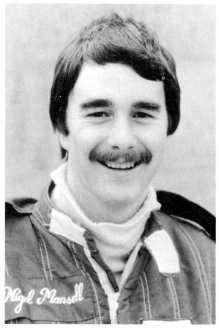

The face tells a tale across a decade
and a half of motor racing.

'I'm a race engineer. At the race meeting you work with the driver and the other engineers to get the most out of the performance of the car: to make it go quickly and reliably. Also you get involved in the tactics of the race, the pit stops, all the technical aspects of the car and setting it up. The set-up is getting the performance out of the car, isn't it?'

This business of setting a car up is constantly discussed and, evidently, some drivers are better at it than others, but what it is really?

'Every circuit is different in the amount of wing you need to run to make a quick lap time — its surface, the type of corners, whether it's heavy on brakes, heavy on the tyres, heavy on the engine. So you have your package of bits supplied by the factory, which are different wing settings, different springs, different roll bars — how high you sometimes run the car — and gear ratios. You can change those to alter the characteristics of the car. It means that while you have your "basic" car, and it will always be that car, you can "point" it in one

Sharing a joke with Jean-Marie Balestre, once President of FISA, the governing body.

direction or the other to improve it. You need a great deal of driver input. We have a lot of data recording systems which tell us a lot about the way the car is operating, but we don't really have many things which can tell us whether the car is any better or not. We can say that this particular characteristic has been changed by this particular percentage. You need a driver to say well, actually it feels worse.

'Nigel was very good at that, very decisive, very good at saying this is better or this is worse; very good at not saying, "Aaah, I'm not really sure, I'm in two minds". No, he'd say it was better or worse. Because he drove the car one hundred per cent all of the time, he'd ask "Which was my quickest lap?", and you'd tell him and he'd say, "Well, that must be the best set-up, mustn't it?" Next, you put something else on the car, modify it in another way. He'd go out and do another few laps, come in and say, "Well, that was quicker still, wasn't it? It must be better, then." That's how we went testing.'

Your evaluation of Mansell as a driver to work with?

'I found him very, very easy [see McGee, Chapter Three]. I got to know him quite well and I took the trouble to make sure that if he made some comment like I could do with a bit out of the seat here, the next time he sat in the car it was right [Brown wasn't making an ironical prod at McLaren].

'He always wanted to be surrounded by people who were what he would describe as positive: for instance, if we were second on the grid, people who'd want to be first, not people who'd say "Ah, well, we're second, that's bloody good". He thought, "No, it isn't any good because I aim to be first". He wanted to be surrounded by people who wanted to be — or were — as competitive as he was: because the race meeting began Friday morning ten o'clock, as it then was, and it was world domination from that point onwards. You had to go out and be quicker by as big a margin as possible than anybody else for the rest of the weekend. He also understood, however, that you win the race as slowly as you can, which, of course, is the trick in order to make your car survive the rigours of the race.

'To work with a guy like that was exciting. Every time he got in the car, you thought, yes, this is going to be interesting. We'll see what you make of this. If for some reason the time didn't come, he'd say I had a bit of a problem with this or that or I had traffic or I'm afraid, David, the car won't go quick enough, we'll have to work at it. He would not say the car isn't quick enough, that's it and I'm off. He'd say it's not quick enough and what can we do about it?' The radio seems to be a significant tool for you and the driver. Speak to me about that, please.

'On the radio he used to sing a little bit, mainly in 1987. In the race we had a nursery rhyme once! We also had "Here we go, here we go, here we go" once. He'd move into a state of concentration and just get on with it, round and round and round, and then suddenly he'd ask something like "How you doing in the pit lane?", and he'd switch the radio off again and we'd be saying "What did he say? What did he say?" He'd do that when things were going well. The nursery rhyme was just giving us something to worry about, really. You can imagine him thinking right, I'll get them going, I'll give them a nursery rhyme.

'He used to talk about getting a "wake-up call". "We'll do 20 laps and if things are going well I want you to come on the radio and tell me that my position is so-and-so rather than just show me the pit board." Mind you, in Spain one year the mirror came off and hit him on the side of the crash helmet before I was due to give him his "wake-up call" and he came over the radio saying I don't want to be woken up! There were moments when it was quite funny . . .'

But it wasn't all like that, was it?

'We had a bit of an altercation when the gearbox packed up on the grid in the rain at Imola [in 1991]. He wasn't very impressed by that. He got left on the grid, no first or second gear, so he was stuck in neutral. He was engulfed by the pack, which must have been a bloody frightening experience even for a guy who'd been there before. Then he set off and Brundle ran into the back of him coming into the chicane, so eventually he'd done one lap and he was well upset about that. He got very outright. It was all recorded by a FOCA video, without sound, the arms waving, the shouting. That's forgivable because you knew the guy was going to take the car by the scruff of the neck and go and do the business.'

I've always felt Mansell was a creative driver, in the sense that he could make things happen from unlikely circumstances. Your evaluation of Mansell the driver?

Right *Pedal power, and enjoying it. Note the Red Five.*

Experimenting with angles.
This is Canada, 1992.

It always does seem a waste, unless you've won.

'Very much an opportunist when it came to overtaking, which all the best drivers are. You tend not to be a successful driver if you sit round behind the others because they all get away. There were times when he did overtaking manoeuvres which made you draw your breath in, but he used to get away with them. He got caught out in Montreal in 1992, but there were very few occasions like that. He'd go for the intimidation if he was behind somebody, try and intimidate them into doing something wrong — as you would. He wouldn't just sit there politely behind. The idea was to get in front and he would try absolutely everything he could think of to do that. If it had been a lesser driver than Senna in those last laps at Monaco in 1992, they

172

might well have been intimidated into a mistake. The thing is, when you've this Red Five flashing left and right in your mirrors it's very difficult to concentrate on what's ahead . . .'

That time at Monaco was almost role-reversal. In general Senna out-psyched or intimidated everyone else, particularly in qualifying, where they scampered out of his way, or races like Monaco, where they scampered out of his way when he came up to lap them.

'I don't think Nigel had fear of Ayrton, like a lot of drivers did. In common with most top drivers, he had a lot of respect for the other guy's ability — because Ayrton was so successful and obviously quick — but Nigel wasn't frightened of him, wasn't frightened of anybody. That was the thing, really. He was as good, if not better, than everybody else so he was capable of beating them. It wasn't a question of "Oh dear, here comes that guy with the yellow helmet in a McLaren behind me".'

It takes us to lap five of the Spanish Grand Prix at Barcelona in 1991 when Mansell and Senna, the two most ferocious practitioners of Formula 1, went wheel-to-wheel at 180 mph-plus down the straight and at one instant, when Brown and the rest of the world drew breath in, the distance between them measured millimetres and closing.

'That was two guys both in competitive cars, both driving exactly as Formula 1 should be driven by everybody: very quickly and with respect for each other's safety but neither giving way. If either had refused to compete with the other they weren't doing their job properly. They were both there to compete with each other and they did, and they did. *That's* what it's about.'

Nigel Mansell's Career Statistics

P = pole; FL = fastest lap; R = retired; DNS = did not start

1980   Three GPs (Lotus), no finishes.

1981   13 GPs (Lotus), highest 3, championship 14.

1982   13 GPs (Lotus), highest 3, championship 14.

1983   15 GPs (Lotus), highest 3, championship 12.

1984   16 GPs (Lotus), highest 3, championship 9.

1985   16 GPs (Williams), two wins, championship 6.

1986   16 GPs (Williams), five wins, championship 2.

1987   14 GPs (Williams), six wins, championship 2.

1988   14 GPs (Williams), highest 2, championship 9.

1989   15 GPs (Ferrari), two wins, championship 4.

1990   16 GPs (Ferrari), one win, championship 5.

1991   16 GPs (Williams), five wins, championship 2.

1992 (Williams-Renault)

1 Mar	South Africa	P/FL/1
22 Mar	Mexico	P/1
5 Apr	Brazil	P/1
3 May	Spain	P/FL/1
17 May	San Marino	P/1
31 May	Monaco	P/FL/2
14 June	Canada	R
5 July	France	P/FL/1
12 July	Britain	P/FL/1
26 July	Germany	P/1
16 Aug	Hungary	FL/2
30 Aug	Belgium	P/2
13 Sept	Italy	P/FL/R
27 Sept	Portugal	P/1
25 Oct	Japan	P/FL/R
8 Nov	Australia	P/R

Championship: Mansell 108, Patrese 56,
Schumacher 53, Senna 50, Berger 49, Brundle 38.

1993 (Newman-Haas Lola IndyCar)

21 Mar	Australia	P/1
4 Apr	Phoenix	DNS
18 Apr	Long Beach	P/3
30 May	Indianapolis	3
6 June	Milwaukee	1
13 June	Detroit	P/R
27 June	Portland	P/2
11 July	Cleveland	3
18 July	Toronto	R
1 Aug	Michigan	1
8 Aug	New Hampshire	P/1
22 Aug	Wisconsin	2
29 Aug	Vancouver	6
12 Sept	Mid-Ohio	P/12
19 Sept	Nazareth	P/1

3 Oct Laguna Seca   R

Championship: Mansell 191, Emerson Fittipaldi 183, Paul Tracy 157, Bobby Rahal 133, Raul Boesel 132, Mario Andretti 117.

Other race:
31 Oct Donington
     TOCA Shoot-out
     (Ford Mondeo)   R

1994 (Newman-Haas Lola IndyCar;
Williams Renault for France, Europe, Japan, Australian GPs)

Date	Location	Result
20 Mar	Australia	P/9
10 Apr	Phoenix	3
17 Apr	Long Beach	2
29 May	Indianapolis	R
5 June	Milwaukee	5
12 June	Detroit	P/R
26 June	Portland	5
3 July	French GP	R
10 July	Cleveland	2
17 July	Toronto	R
31 July	Michigan	P/R
14 Aug	Mid-Ohio	7
21 Aug	New Hampshire	R
4 Sept	Vancouver	10
11 Sept	Winsconsin	13
18 Sept	Nazareth	R
9 Oct	Laguna Seca	8
16 Oct	European GP	R
6 Nov	Japanese GP	4
13 Nov	Australian GP	P/1

IndyCar Championship, eighth, 88; Formula 1 Championship, ninth, 14.

1995 (McLaren Mercedes)

Date	Location	Result
30 Apr	San Marino	10
14 May	Spain	R